Drops of Jules

Julia Grigorian

Eliezer Tristan Publishing
Portland, OR

Cover design by Aaron Smith

To my Dad;

When a week into college I called you, lost and distraught over choosing a major, you had but one soft reply. With that logical mind of yours, you said, "You like to write. Be an English major."

As though it was that simple.

Then, it was.

This is for you.

Table of Contents

Disclaimer

Foreword: *"I wanted something to consume me instead of the pain and eating disorders are all-consuming."*

FROM MY OWN EXPERIENCE *with an eating disorder, I can tell you this; they are all-consuming. I wanted something to consume me instead of the pain that I felt.*

Do not let me be misunderstood; this was not on purpose. Eating disorders slowly weasel their way in. They often start with some tiny, clueless thought or behavior that you'd have no idea would lead to a descent into this world of madness. Before you know it, you're there, in an abyss of seemingly perpetual suffering.

To say the least, it's tough to escape. The disorder becomes an addiction, an abuser, and somehow...a friend. The one thing that is always there. The replacement for you, your identity, and your pain.

Julia's story is one that helped me personally and will continue to help many. Long before we ever spoke, I was an avid reader of Julia's blog. When it was closed, I sometimes went to the web address to see if, by chance, it'd be back up. I know that some of you out there did the same thing. Now, you have this book. I can tell you that it was more than worth the wait.

Whether you are a first-time reader or one that has been following Julia for quite some time as I have, I know that this story will teach you something. Julia's words are powerful, as is her story. She is immensely intelligent and wise beyond her years, offering new ideas and saying what others won't. I'm honored to work with someone so talented and perceptive. Writing about privilege, travel, and the truths about recovery, this is a title that you can't miss.

I will always treasure my copy of this book. I know that everyone else who finds it in their hands will, too.

-Sparklle Rainne, Editor and Friend

THIS IS NOT A STORY FOR EVERYONE. This is a story that is unsettling, but it is true. Everything that rests here on these pages is what led me to the woman I am today. It is not the best story in the world, but I have the blessing of sharing my story, so here it is.

It's not for everyone. But, it is for me.

This book, and my words, are not a replacement for medical professionals. This book does not substitute treatment. My story and my experience are not universal. I do not expect my recovery to resonate with everyone who reads these words. Likely, most will not find any semblance of a relation between my recovery story and his or her own. This goes to only further prove how uniquely nuanced and yet remarkably similar each person's eating disorders are.

I want to and need to begin by recognizing my privilege in this world as a white, cisgendered, heterosexual woman with an eating disorder. I was raised in a middle-class family. I wanted for nothing. My family supported me endlessly. I don't have student loans looming over me. Only now in this past year have I been on my own financially. Even now, if I had a sudden desperate need for something and didn't have the funds, I know my family could step in. I recognize that the majority of the world comes nowhere near that level of comfort.

For others, eating disorder recovery requires a constant search for funds for food, whereas I was plagued with countless fear foods but had items that felt "safe" to eat. It was a done deal. My parents bought them for me. No questions asked. Others don't have it like this. Others struggle to find food to eat. Food insecurity plagues the world in so many different facets, and I was lucky and privileged enough not to have to engage in this issue while struggling to overcome anorexia.

Not once in my life have I had the burden of explaining my identity to anyone. In America, being white, straight, and female is socially acceptable. When you are a person of color, a member LGBTQIA+ community, a part of a stigmatized religious community, or anyone who isn't automatically given acceptance by our society, you are often expected to justify your identity multiple times a day in order for society to even begin to accept you. I have never lived that experience. When I was in the depths of my eating disorder, I had it "easy." I didn't have to focus on anything related to my identity and could pay attention exclusively to getting well. I didn't have to worry about where my next meal was coming from, I had the luxury of eating "safe food" and I wasn't working forty hours a week while going to school, unlike many people who don't have that option. I didn't have any religious rituals involving fasting to navigate. Rarely did I have people criticize me or make fun of me. In fact, I was surrounded by a bounty of support, though I didn't want it at the time.

I have so much privilege in this world; it breaks me. I wish I could give it away. I did absolutely nothing to earn my place in this world. I had this privileged life handed to me. I do my utmost to extend all the gratitude in the world for it, but I know I can do more.

Please know that I recognize my privilege and that it is so unfair.

I feel fraudulent in claiming that my life is one of struggle. I know people out there have it so much worse. I really do know that. I know that to others, the idea of someone like me having an eating disorder and it being "so hard" is absurd. *Oh no, poor little white girl who has nothing else to do but worry about her vanity and be so preoccupied with how she looks.*

Eating disorders are so much more than that, though. They can affect anyone, anywhere, at any time. They sneak up on you, and oftentimes… you don't realize what's going on until you're in too deep.

All my life, my free time has catered to storytelling, whether it be through reading or writing. I dream up novels, waking up in the middle of the night, jotting down gibberish in the hopes I'll recall the vision I had in my broken slumber. In me resides fiction clawing at my fingers, asking to be written down.

This book is not a sum of fairy tales and imaginative descriptions that are meant to leave you, kind reader, captivated. This is a story that does not gradually lead you into the rising actions, the crisis, the dénouement. This is a story that jumps right in because I don't want to leave anyone with a trace of romanticism. This is the raw core of my eating disorder. Some of it will sound trivial. Some of it you may read and wonder, *"really? That upset you?"* For that, you are entirely valid.

While my eating disorder happened to me, it also happened *because of m*e. I recognize I am not pardoned of guilt or fault. It is my hope to display how mental illness is a combination of both external factors and one's own actions. The chapters that follow will not contain eloquent prose, for that would only act as a disservice to the true lived experience of an eating disorder. Do not walk into this book expecting a joyous read, but do expect the truth—

the truth as well as one can address something so complex in the limited expression of the English language.

I want to examine mental illness, specifically anorexia, from the inside out. I want to show how easily it is to seep into it. I want to explore how eating disorders are not about aesthetics for the majority of people. It stems from deeper issues. In my case, sexual trauma, but for others, it could be something entirely different. This is my story, my struggle, and my experience.

These words and my journey are not universal for everyone, nor do I expect my recovery to resonate with everyone who reads this.

I want to discuss the effect other people had on my recovery, both negatively and positively. In time past, one of the most often asked questions I receive is, *"How can I help someone I love?"* I don't always have the answer for that, but I can examine what people did and said to me, in the hopes it might incite a response for anyone in this position. Combined with this, I want to make it clear that everyone who struggles with an eating disorder is still a person underneath the murky prison cell of his or her mind. Every living being on this earth is inherently unique in the most honest and true way, and only after did I begin to appreciate the utter beauty of our diverse world did I see the importance of community and supporting one another. Ultimately, this is what drove me to the final stages of recovery where I linger today.

Finally, I want to work through the multidimensional process of recovery, displaying how it's not just about eating more food and gaining weight, but rather reinventing my life narrative in a way that is not defined nor limited to the restriction my life was guided by for long.

I don't know what brought you here today, sitting up somewhere perched against a pillow, absorbing my words. I don't know why you chose me and my story. I want to give you a resounding thank you. If even a sentence of my life makes you see eating disorders a bit clearer, I have done my job. Whatever tragedy befell onto you, landing you here; my heart aches for the pain in your life.

Always know that there is hope. That is my final goal here; to leave you with hope. Hope doesn't always pan out, but I can promise you this; hope is the very thing you need when an eating disorder plagues on.

Cheers to you. There is hope. Thank you for joining me here today.

Trigger warning: *this book contains calories, weight, disordered exercise behaviors and disordered eating behaviors. It describes sexual assault and rape. If you have experienced any of these things and do not feel well enough to read about them, please be cautious in continuing with this work. Julia Grigorian is not a medical or mental health professional and is not offering medical or mental health advice through this book. This is her story and she hopes to help other survivors enter recovery and to know that they are never alone.*

Do not use this book to indulge your eating disorder. You know what I am talking about. Please, be mindful in reading this book.

Gorilla thighs.

MY OLDER BROTHER AND I were born to two loving, selfless parents. Throughout my life, we always had a cat or two bustling around our home. I was born in Sacramento, California, but when I was six years old, we moved to the Los Angeles area to a city called Glendale. That is where I grew up and lived out this story until I moved to San Diego for college.

My family was everything and anything a child could ask for. Financially, we never struggled. Extracurriculars always were made available to me. My parents love each other more today than they did when they first married. My brother and I rarely fought. I had it easy. I was lucky. I was blessed. I still am.

When we moved to Glendale, my parents put my brother and me in a small, private Christian school. This school went from Kindergarten all the way to twelfth grade. During elementary and middle school, I enjoyed my time there immensely. I accepted Jesus Christ into my heart, though I knew nothing of what that truly entailed. Christianity was the only spiritual concept introduced to me, and I found comfort in it as a young child. Who could expect an eight-year-old to comprehend the gravity of such a decision? To this day, I could never articulate the true form of my religious identity. This is largely the reason why I ultimately decided to earn my degree in religious studies, but I'll revisit that topic at a later time.

After watching the Summer Olympics at four years old, I wanted to become a gymnast. Immediately my parents enrolled me, and I loved it. Learning and achieving new skills empowered my little self. Exploring new ways to move my body exhilarated and empowered me. From an early age, I knew what it felt like to be strong. One might think that wearing leotards daily sets one up for a healthy dose of insecurity, but because I started so young, I had not the faintest idea. I never felt self-conscious of my body because the issue never arose.

The day before my eleventh birthday, I experienced my first period. I look back on that day now fondly. I saw the movie "Hairspray" with my mother. Just before the film began, we set off to the bathroom where I discovered my birthday gift. I remember looking down, squatted on the toilet and calling out to my mother. She came into the stall ecstatic and so proud of me. I remember staring up at her dumbfounded at her excitement. I was horrified. I don't remember anything about the movie because I just sat in the theatre *feeling* my body. This is the first instance in my childhood where I realized that I existed inside of a body. Everything prior felt two-dimensional.

Passing through my first menstrual cycle changed everything for me. I noticed my body more, and my curiosity about bodily functions piqued. I spent more time looking in the mirror. Initially, it was not for critiquing, but more so plain observations. Still, I noticed parts of my body that were not as great as I once thought them to be, but I recognize that that's completely normal and valid for any young girl going through puberty.

Middle school started, and it was a fantastic change of pace from the monotonous days of grade school where you stay in the same seat all day, every day. As a child, I intrinsically knew the world was expansive, and I wanted to participate in any way I could. Having the movement of interacting and learning in different classes fueled me in a new and enjoyable way. I raced from class to class every forty-five minutes and loved all of the exposure I got to different teachers.

People who meet me now are utterly gobsmacked at who I was as a child. Though I certainly am talkative again now; I am nowhere near the level of extroverted-ness that I was growing up. My gregarious spirit defined me as a child. I bounced from person to person, talking about whatever floated into my mind. Some have wagered that becoming an adult calms the internal voice within all of us. True; that could very well have been the nature of my personality's journey as I matured. Undoubtedly, though, my eating disorder quieted me.

Throughout my middle school years, my weight rested above a socially approved number for a female of my age and height. AKA, the people in my life considered my body "chubby." In no way was I an unhealthy weight, but rather, upon reflection, I was at the exact size my body needed to be at. Given that I started menstruation at such a young age, my body was in the process of figuring itself out. Whereas the girls around me still pranced around in lanky, straightened bodies, I swam through new curves and attempted to adjust as so. Only a small fraction of the other girls in my grade were on the same track physically, and subconsciously, I think that we all gravitated toward one another as a silent, "*I understand you.*"

I'd always been what one could consider a "good" eater. I tried new food, I was always up for dessert, and I enjoyed going out to restaurants with family and friends. I was not society's ideal thin and frail young lady. However, I can genuinely say that I was happy and didn't think of my body as "unacceptable." There were details I'd change; I remember standing in front of my mirror watching the under-part of my arms jiggle, but I also remember shrugging it off without a second thought.

I always loved food. My after school daily snack usually consisted of chocolate ice cream drowned in Hershey's chocolate syrup. This would also be my dessert at night, too, if I was feeling especially hungry. I never turned down a brownie or a piece of cake, and Reese's were my weakness. I didn't binge eat nor did I hoard food. I was just a girl who loved to eat, and I placed no judgment around food. My family loved my adventurous taste buds, and they always encouraged me to eat when I needed to. I was raised in a family that did not promote eating disorders whatsoever, and I want to make that very clear. Did I grow up surrounded by disordered behaviors in regards to food? Absolutely, but that is par for the course here in America, so I can't fault anyone around me for my eating disorder. We all have our struggle with food, whether you are the most intuitive eater on the planet or not. We all aren't perfect with food, and sometimes that rubs off on one another.

During middle school, I struggled to maintain good, solid friendships with girls. By going to such a small school (less than one hundred students per grade), nothing was kept secret. People knew every little detail. Girls, myself included, spent every waking moment gossiping, and it was honestly exhausting. I got so tired of it and ended up just giving up on working on those friendships. I wasn't a recluse; but I stopped pushing people to love me. If people liked me, they liked me.

My first bout of doubting my body came in eighth grade, right at the tail end of the school year. My best male friend and I struggled to navigate a friendship with unsettled hormones, emotions, and all around feeling out of synch with one another. Neither of us is to blame, really. Puberty just sucks sometimes. One afternoon, though, we argued over who-knows-what, when he came at me with the insult of calling me "gorilla thighs." Everyone around us erupted in cackles. Did he mean it? No, of course not. He was a twelve-year-old boy trying to prove himself in the world. Did I internalize that fatphobia for the rest of my life, though? You betcha! At the time, I did nothing about it but sob when I had the chance to be alone and sulk in it. Years later, though, when I needed "motivation" to continue on my disordered path, my mind went straight to that instant. To this day, I can only wear skinny jeans when I'm having a really good day.

After he said it, one of the girls in the group called him out on it, noting that it was out of character for the minor dispute we were having, but the damage was done.

Tears swelled down my face, as I just felt so hopeless. The one guy that I shared everything with had called me an animal.

I went home that day begging my mind to stop. His words played over and over again on a loop, but I didn't have the capability of stopping it. This was the first time I felt out of control with my own thoughts. All I knew was that I needed it to stop. I called his cell phone. It rang and rang. Ignored. I tried again. Ignored. On the third call, he picked up, told me never to call again because I was not worth his energy and he hoped my fat self would die. Again, we were eighth graders. We were children. I'm not holding him accountable for this a decade later. I recognize completely that these words carried no weight, and we've worked through it at this point in our lives. He is married and has a beautiful family. I wish him all the best. I really, honestly do. I don't blame him, but those words festered in me, the seeds awaiting the sprouting of damage to come a few years later.

Graduation the next day meant formal attire, plenty of pictures, and attention on myself within my family. Back in early spring, my mom and I dotted about in the mall, in search of the perfect dress for the occasion. It was the first time I was to take part in a celebration for my own achievements. Though graduation was a formality of sorts, one that everyone is gifted, my mom took it to be a special occasion, worthy of a fun day shopping with one another. We took our time going through various shops as we evaluated lace and tulle and shades and sparkles; shopping heaven for the pair of us. When we stumbled into our final store of the day, already eyeing an emerald green gown elsewhere, we landed upon a deep magenta gown with simple black brocade lace and beading dispersed throughout the underlay. I put it on and watched as my mom's eyes lit up. She told me I looked beautiful, and I looked at myself in the mirror. I remember looking at my mom through the mirror, back to myself, and recalling how much I looked like her.

When I think about the people in my life who molded me, the first characteristic I consider is the person's relationship toward food. In my head, I crafted a list years ago, ranking the people in my life based on his or her relationship to food. Only now do I understand this as a symptom of my eating disorder, but in the early stages of recovery, this was a tool guiding me toward intuitive eating.

In a world of people held captive by dieting, my mother held her own quite well. This is not to say there were never diet products in the house, because I grew up watching my mom drink slim fast and eat lean cuisine. In her normal routine, she exercised for an hour a day, usually something light like the elliptical. She was not immune to the pressure of society weighing on her to maintain a certain physique. That said, she also did not let these norms control her life. When she wanted wine, she poured a glass. When she had a craving for something sweet after dinner, she was able to have one piece of chocolate and feel satisfied. Other nights, she could have cookies and milk and feel fine. I never heard her utter words of guilt about herself. In recent years, she's made a few comments in reference to herself, but I don't think those words hit anyone else's radar apart from my own, and that is only because I am particularly sensitive to such remarks.

Growing up, my mom never forced me to diet or slim down. There are three conversations I can remember in my entire life when she commented on my body before my eating disorder. They all stick out to me because I remember them hurting, but also recognizing that what she told me was always something she was relaying from others. Each time, it was someone from my external family, a great uncle, a grandmother, a cousin, making a reference about my body weight to my mom, who then shared this with me. On the third occasion, I was thirteen years old, helping myself to homemade guacamole when my mom pulled me aside. She picked up a chip, scooped guacamole, and told me she thought this was a more proper chip-to-dip ratio. Apparently, I took too much on each scoop.

"It'll still taste as good, but it won't be as much food. Just watch how much you're eating."

"Oh," I recall replying. "Okay."

With a chip already in my hand, I speculated my next action. Unsure, I waited her out, knowing she'd pop along to a different conversation. As soon as she did, I set the chip down on a napkin and folded into the couch, my appetite gone. I ate a minimal amount of a dinner that I usually loved. We were at my grandparent's house, filled with the spices of Armenian food. My favorite meal, but I could only think about that chip.

None of this is to say my mom created an eating disorder for me out of one stupid guacamole comment, because she did not. My family had nothing to do with my eating disorder. If anything, they are remarkably intuitive eaters, especially my brother. I showcase this instance because it serves as an example of how nuanced and subtle diet culture is. My mom meant no harm by such a comment. If anything, she was protecting me from my relatives coming to me directly. Those interactions, as I imagine, only would have been filled with harsh sentiments veiled under the guise of love. Apart from those few times, before my eating disorder, my mom was the reason why I had such confidence within me. Before my eating disorder, I was a gregarious, social butterfly, ready to take on anything and everything.

So, when it came to that graduation day when I was thirteen years old, I pushed away those thoughts as best as I could, knowing what my mom saw in me. I really tried my best.

All throughout my life, though I've swayed and drowned in society's beauty standards, I have always known my mother to be the most beautiful human being in the world. For me to feel as though I had a semblance of that same beauty within me—indescribable. This was my dress, and I remember staring at it every night, anxiously awaiting the real day.

But then, the day came, and I stared at the gown with hesitation. I resented the spaghetti straps. I abhorred the length, only hitting to mid-thigh. Conservatively appropriate, but with recent remarks, I felt that it showed too much of my figure. Knowing the teenage version of myself, had what transpired never came to be, I easily would have put the gown on first thing the morning of my graduation, but instead, I left it to only five minutes before. I curled my hair, all the while staring at the gown in the corner of my mirror.

Sitting in my desk chair, I gawked at the face reflected back at me through the mirror. I took the moment to understand that this was a face I'd not always seen. I understood that my life grew me into this face. At early ages, I looked at a softer face, one with less freckles, different teeth, fuller cheeks. I understood not only the ability for a face to evolve but also the body's malleability. Just as my thin, lifeless hair transforms into voluminous curls with the help of a hot iron, I could also alter other parts of me if I chose.

Middle school graduation came and went without any focus on the academic achievement—at least for myself. All night, I avoided the pictures, the smiles, the hugs. I felt ashamed of anyone hugging me, lest they feel the extra layer of fat coating my body. Even still, though I'd no previous experience feeling this way, something within me knew this was my time to put on a show. This was my act. No one could even hint at the idea of the thoughts ricocheting around my mind. No one could know how huge I felt. Instead, I focused on others, taking each of my friends and commenting on her beauty, her luster, her expert decision making in choosing the right dress for herself. Internal hatred, outward appreciation. It's how it's always worked for me.

Welled up tears lodged behind my eyelids all night, but I made it through. At the corner of my eye, I looked at my old friend who said the comment, the one who made me question my beauty. I wasn't mad at him; I didn't know I even had a right to be. I just missed him. I loved him. I still do love him. I just wanted him to love me back. Not in a specific way. Just in a human way. I wanted him to look at me and share a laugh with me as we always had. That night, when I peered at him, stealing a hidden glance on occasion, I wanted to know what he thought of me that day; if there was an ounce of love left in him for me. Instead, when I walked past him, I wondered if he thought I looked like a different animal today. It consumed me, shadowing what otherwise should have been a celebratory memory to cherish.

Following this, I kept that idea of changing my body strapped into a corner of my head, though I did little about it. Summer propelled me into a time of fulfillment and joy. I had more time for gymnastics, and I also spent the days volunteering with children. During this summer, I learned how pure a child's love for someone can be. I learned I had that intuitive craving to have children of my own one day. Up until that point, it was always an assumption of mine to have children. It was the life narrative I'd grown up with, seeing as my mom loved her role in my life. She was good at it, too. Having that in my life made the decision for wanting motherhood easy, but only following this summer did I happen upon that realization from within. Children are forgiving, audacious, and looking for companionship in anyone they encounter. Children have no agenda in conversations. Being surrounded by that during a time when I just as easily could have sunken into a depressive state of isolation is what saved me from tripping downhill too early in life. Had I sunk into anorexia when I was thirteen years old, who knows where I would be today.

Gymnastics was always a healthy atmosphere for me until years later. When I was thirteen, though, gymnastics was the central location for positive body image. I know many gymnasts and coaches struggle with eating disorders and demonizing athletes for weight, but my coaches always supported strength. Having larger thighs meant vigor, it meant working hard toward goals, it meant dedication. Larger thighs had no correlation to shame—they were something to take pride in.

The first semester of freshman year swirled by in a haze of transition and excitement. Opting out of P.E., I tried out for the volleyball team—a feat of which required only mere effort to make the freshman team. Hardly anyone on the team exhibited skill, but we all had a grand time trying. Originally, the team was coached by my former fourth grade teacher (that's just how private schools work). When she unexpectedly needed surgery at the beginning of the season, she tapped out in favor of her two assistant coaches taking over. Both of them were former alumni who played on the boy's volleyball team throughout their time at the same school, hedging their bets at a nearby college, and making the most of a part-time gig that clearly gave them a chance to practice their beloved sport. The season taught me nothing about the actual sport, but it was a season to forever and always remember. Although I'd hoped the positive body image gymnastics gifted me would transfer over to volleyball, tiny spanx became a trap of which I drowned in comparisons, cellulite, and wedgies.

One weekend during this year, a friend threw a pool party, inviting most of the grade. This majority included my former best friend who'd dubbed me, "gorilla thighs." Other than my own mind, no one even remembered the altercation. A summer does that to the teenage mind, blurring away the drama of a former being who once you called yourself. Even the boy himself gave way to the idea we'd moved passed anything, at least externally. Personally, I knew we'd crossed a boundary never to mend. Previously, we'd enlisted ourselves in a constant, ceaseless string of text messages, bouncing random ideas off one another, picking the thought up after one of us fell asleep the night before. This didn't exist any longer, but no one was the wiser apart from the two of us. Others were blind to the separation the two of us had, but I myself felt the aching void every day when I looked at him. What he and I had before was as intimate and trusting as two young teenagers could platonically create.

When I arrived at the pool party, I awkwardly stripped down to my bathing suit and slipped into the pool in one fluid motion, minimizing the seconds my body shed exposed to the world. Gradually, as more people arrived, groups formed and settled, and a line around the diving board developed. With insecurities seeping in through every crevice of my mind, I knew a diving board was actually a place I was competent. I took my turn and flipped into the pool. I remembered the confident feeling of soaring through the air, the same thrill that kept me practicing gymnastics for years and years.

When I came up for air, I broke through the water's surface just as that same boy, my old dear friend, uttered, "big splash." It poured out of his mouth accompanied by a sinful grin. We locked eyes as his sight quivered; he'd not meant for me to hear that. But I had. His face filled with a combination of cynicism, pleasure, and guilt. Instinctively, I knew that the guilt I saw on his face was not out of regretting the comment, but having been caught for it. Around me, shudders of laughter hindered any chance I had at an eloquent response.

I excused myself to the bathroom where I had what I now clearly recognize as a panic attack. At the time, I felt like I was experiencing what I'd always imagined a heart attack to be like.

The emotions rushing through my heart were so heavy. A growing ache shot itself into my chest, and I fell to the floor. I tried to get back up, but I was crippled. It took any energy I was capable of harnessing in me to turn my cries into silent sobs, heaving over myself. My thoughts got away from me. Another voice began articulating my needs and wants, almost in a different language, but one I inherently knew.

While in the bathroom, time for me didn't exist. If I'd guessed, I would have thought I spent under ten minutes attempting to compose myself. When I finally managed to reduce the blotchy skin around my eyes enough to where it could be mistaken as a sunburn, I re-joined the party. As I came back outside, I heard the traditional birthday melody tarnished by rowdy teenage voices. Everyone gathered around a Costco sheet cake, oddly my favorite, as the birthday boy blew out his candles. It was a marvelous, decadent cake, with almost as much frosting as pastry itself; a cake that never touched my mouth. I sat there too ashamed of my body to allow myself anything.

My mom picked me up shortly thereafter, en route to gymnastics practice. I did not say one word to her the entire thirty minute drive, a rarity for me. I grew up gregarious, busting at the bits to talk to anyone and everyone about whatever popped into my mind. She inquired about my silence, but I shrugged her off, announcing I was tired from a day out in the sun, hoping to conserve my energy for practice.

Minutes later, I arrived at the gym. When the door opened and the familiar waft of sweat mixed with chalk filled my nostrils, the tears came streaming. My brother spotted me within seconds and ran over to me. Prior to this day, he and I were always close, but never connected on an emotional level. Never was he the one I opened up to, but intuitively we knew were always there for one another. That day though, he took one look at me, sobbing away and ran over to me. He just held me for the longest time. For me, this is the moment I look back on in my life and realize what pure, unconditional love is. He didn't ask me any questions. He just stood there and hugged me, all the while there must have been thirty or so people around the gym looking in on us. Eventually, I gulped a few sentences out, giving him the briefest of explanations. My brother clasped my face in between his hands and said to me, "Julia, you are absolutely beautiful. Absolutely beautiful." He then went on to say few profane comments about the boy, in an attempt likely to make me laugh.

We stood there for ten minutes while I drenched his shirt in my salty tears and he stroked my hair.

I moved on from that day. This boy is not the reason why anorexia latched onto me. Potentially though, it planted the seeds. Perhaps, anyway. There is no way to be sure. Lots of little moments in my life led up to the ultimate demise of my eating disorder, but when I look back on the memories that defeated me, these spring up as the early ones.

The problem with a memoir lies in the dilemma of painting with broad strokes, intermixed with complex patterns the amateur artist I was at the time would not have understood, as though I had an eye staring straight into my future, looking down the barrel of the gun, waiting for it to trigger. But, I was in front of a blocked wall. Any connections I make now only occur in the present. As I managed my way through every step of this journey, I refused to see the connections. I only make them now. This event sticks out to me as planting the seeds, but who could ever really know? Did I know it then? Not at all. But it happened, and it hurt, so it is here for you to make sense of, kind reader.

I get it. No one wants to talk about rape.

ALL RIGHT. TOGETHER, LET'S TAKE A collective sigh before we delve into this chapter. Yes, I realize this entire book is about mental illness and suffering and depression, but right now I am going to tell you the story of how I was raped multiple times as a fourteen-year-old girl. Yes, we are going to do it. Together. We are going to knead out the hidden parts of my story. On occasion, I shared aspects of this story in small doses, always choosing to hold back select moments or conversations. But this is my opportunity to change the very part of my story that, for so long, I felt I had no control over.

Sexual abuse is rampant. Just because I'm choosing to focus my story on when I was raped does not mean this is my only bout with sexual assault. A man once grabbed my vaginal area in the parking lot on my way home from work. I couldn't tell you the number of times someone has slapped my butt and chuckled. God forbid I'm having a rough day, because that usually lends itself to a man taking the opportunity to remind me to "smile more" and "use this pretty face of mine."

If I'm being honest, I realized for so long I didn't want to share this part of my story for two reasons: one being the obvious stigma I receive from using my voice in this manner. I already have the label of "anorexic," so it's not that easy slapping on, "rape victim." It took me seven years to understand that I'm playing into the flawed system by doing this. I have spent far too long breaking the barriers of society to falter in such a clear and vital part of my story. I am nothing but hypocritical if I choose to only speak out about my anorexia and subsequent recovery, but let the story of my assaults fall to the wayside.

The other reason why I refrained from writing this out for so long was, for some absurd reason, I felt compelled to protect him. Yes, as I'm typing that out I realize that is bullshit. I get it. But when you're fourteen years old and a man in authority tells you something is right and special, you don't get the chance to question it. You just don't. Because if you do, you only blame yourself. I know that's not fair. I recognize that now. That's why I need to write this down.

Still, just as it was with my eating disorder, there is no guidebook on how to write this out. Hence why I am now on my fourth paragraph of the chapter without giving you one detail. Rape is isolating and traumatic, infiltrating every inch of the skin I live in. Not a day goes by when I don't look at myself in the mirror and remember those days. I'll never forget how loud the air around me felt, how the sounds of the world faded away and all I remembered was the scratchy noise of grunts from a man, turned coach, turned stranger, turned monster.

I sit here at twenty-two years old and realize that the man who raped me was this age. I was fourteen at the time. Something about that breaks me.

Okay, I've lingered enough. Let's get to it.

When I was fourteen years old, I joined the school's volleyball team. With no experience, I was awful. I didn't quite care though. It was a nice change of pace from gymnastics, but I knew I was nothing special at the sport.

Our freshman team had two young male coaches, both of which were charismatic, jolly, and overall in it for the easy paycheck and chance to swing a ball around. One of the coaches took a vested interest in a few of us, always ensuring that we had rides home after practice or that we had enough water to make it through the afternoon. At the time, I thought nothing of it, other than he cared for all of us. Our volleyball season happened during the fall when the dark of the night fell before our practice got out, so it made sense for someone in authority to linger around until all of us were headed home. On one evening, my ride was running late, but my coach had somewhere to be. He gave me his number and requested I shoot him a text once my ride picked me up, so he could rest assured I was okay. He came across endearing, concerned. Coming from someone years older than me, charming and handsome, nothing about this set me off. I was flattered.

Over time, my coach shot me the occasional text, sometimes during school hours and sometimes late at night. It gradually grew where, at the time, I never even noticed the difference. The line where it turned inappropriate is too blurred for me to pinpoint it now. On my end, it slipped away from me before I had the chance to understand something was wrong. On his end, it was undoubtedly calculated with utter finesse. Once, during the middle of practice, I checked my phone on a water break and noticed a text from my coach remarking that my "ass looked amazing in my spanx today." Then, thankfully, a pang of panic fluttered in me. I looked over at him, furrowed my brow, giving him a questioning look. He sent another text very quickly apologizing. He also mentioned that he thought of me as a great friend, and at times it was hard to separate that from coaching me. Upon reflection, I don't know if I actually believed that, as naive as I was, or if I was too scared to fight it. I do know that something within me intuitively stitched a notch in my heart to watch out.

A few weeks later, on Valentine's Day, our volleyball team had a match about forty-five minutes away. My parents went away on a trip to celebrate the holiday. They dropped me off at the match, but we coordinated a ride with one of the other girls. When I arrived at the match, I learned that my teammate actually stayed home due to the stomach flu. My parents already left, and the last thing I wanted to do was upset them by ruining their vacation just to drive me back to the house (though I *know* without question they would have). I popped around to every girl on the team asking for rides, when my coach offered a ride home. He let me know he was already taking two of the other girls home, so it wouldn't be that big of a deal. Anxious that I was running out of options, I said a grateful yes. I thought nothing of it, in fact—there were other girls. I knew I also lived the closest, so I'd be the first dropped off. All signs pointed "safe."

With the meet over, I laid on the floor eating a granola bar, talking to my best friend on the team. Teammates dwindled, and I was wrapped up in the conversation with her. I did not realize we were the only two left. Her dad came and picked her up. As I said goodbye to her, I looked around and noticed that it was just the coach and me left. Before I even had the chance to ask, he quickly let me know that some of the girls planned to grab pizza together and one of their parents took over the carpooling for them, leaving just me with a need for a ride.

I'd like to say that, at that moment, I had the foresight to realize something was wrong, but I honestly was just so anxious about burdening anyone in any way, that I succumbed to the only option before me. He made me feel like I had to be grateful for this ride because he was so forthcoming in the offer.

So, I let him take me home.

I knew the way home. I lived there practically my entire life. He went the wrong way. I told him the right way. He didn't change directions. He pulled to the side of the road, moved into an alley, and had his way.

There are no words to describe it. People for centuries have attempted to consolidate experiences with rape into language, but I can tell you that is impossible. Your mind tries to rationalize it every which way, always justifying the rapist's actions in one way or another. This is how my mind learned to screw with me with disordered eating, justifying what I know to be irrational and wrong.

Up, up, down, up, up, down. He gasped. I gasped. Him in ecstasy, I, in agony. A final thrust, he pulled away, wet. He grasped at his calves and heaved. I rolled over to my side, and cowered, staring at nothing. The air smelled sticky with sweat. I learned that semen smelled like an odor my taste buds weren't expected to enjoy yet, like a refined, aged cheese, only for those with years behind them to appreciate a delicacy of such. His cum, like glue, bound the aftermath of us. I inched away from him, but he slapped his hand onto me again, keeping me attached. I let his body linger against mine, and I let my neck fall over the side of the car seat.

I remember hearing the sound of sharpened metal from a short distance away. It soothed me, like when my mother hummed to me as a young child, dreaming me into a lullaby. I felt myself giving over to sleep. I knew I couldn't physically escape, so I let myself mentally, if only for a moment. I dozed, exposed, letting myself forget the one thing I will spend the rest of my life unlearning about myself.

He shook me awake, and I shook myself too. I wiped away my eyes, but they were dry. He twirled a chunk of my matted hair, distressed from the ponytail of the day.

"Can I go home?" I muttered, though I knew it was breath wasted. He was done. He would take me home. For having never gone through it before, I somehow instinctively knew how it worked.

When he dropped me off, I knew my brother was in the house, but I wasn't ready to face anything. I sat on my front porch and watched the plants in the yard. Dragonflies roamed around me, buzzing in the dusky glow. Looking down at my legs, I saw bruises that hadn't existed hours before. I remember the steering wheel puncturing into my back, while he jabbed into me on the front. Twin bruises mapped my hips from him. I sat outside for a few hours, attempting to piece it all together, before going to bed. Disjointed and fragmented. No dinner. I didn't eat for two days. I bled for days following.

It happened again and again. Three times in total. Each in a new spot. New for me, though I am well aware he knew where in the world clandestine caves existed and where it did not. The last happened in a field less than five minutes away from my school. His confidence grew each time. "Fat pig, disgusting creature," he screamed at me, all the while getting off to me. I was a vessel purely for him to rampage, but at the time, I sought worth from this. He spat at me as he told me that was the only proper reaction a vile girl as me deserved.

Before him. I had never seen a penis. He was bubblegum pink. He was flaccid and childish. He was sagging sheath. Up, up, down, up, up, down. He would pull away. I stayed where I was. He moaned occasionally. He braided my hair. He'd complain. He called me names. He asked me questions. I did not answer. He fell asleep. I turned to leave, he fondled me, digging his nails in, marking his territory. My areola bled.

The final time, he didn't take me back to where I needed to be—not school, not home. He left me buried in dust from his words, from pawing, from his twining. My shirt, soaked, I looked down, my nipples plain to see through my drenched uniform. I crawled over to a pine tree, hoping just a moment of shade would cool me off. I put pressure to my breast. I wiped my tears. I confused my hands and the fluids fuse together, a salmon pink. I still think of this as the time when my body felt most united.

After time uncounted, I picked myself and made the short trek back to school, hiding any evidence under a bulky sweatshirt I had with me.

I didn't tell anyone for four years. Two weeks before I graduated high school, I was pulled into the principal's office. This was months into my recovery, when I was in a good place. My body settled at a nice, healthy weight, and my mind felt remarkably clear. Graduation loomed ahead of me, and I just declared my admission to San Diego State. My life was filled with hope. I thought nothing of the summons to the administration building.

When I entered the room, one of my closest friends walked out. As we passed each other, I noticed the blotches all over her skin. She stared down at the floor as she hustled out. I turned away from her to see the dean, the principal, and the assistant principal, circled around the corner of a desk. In front of them lay the school's yearbook for my first year of high school. Glancing down, I saw it opened to the page for my volleyball team with my coach's headshot circled in thick purple marker.

"Hey Julia! How are you this morning?" My principal, chipper as ever, asked me as I stared at the three of them, paralyzed, eyes looked askance. He gestured for me to sit across from them. I looked at the assistant principal and the dean, both women, but neither of them faced me. In front of each them were legal pads with tabs folded over, clearly marked up with information, awaiting more from myself.

They gave me every opportunity to come clean, to be honest, to speak up. But I couldn't do it. I can think of many reasons why, but ultimately, it comes down to the impending shame I felt. I knew the minute words came out

of my mouth, everything would change. With me, I already
carried the label of "anorexic." I couldn't even conceive of
carrying another demerit of sorts. At that point in my life, I
had had enough of change. I was exhausted. That last year
of my life almost killed me, and I couldn't possibly see how
telling the three head people at my school would make
anything in my life improve. I'd managed to keep the
secret for four years, and I felt it could only get easier. I
told myself I just needed to stay collected. If I could
manage that, everything would be okay.

*"Did he ever make you feel uncomfortable? Send you
inappropriate messages? Touch you in a way that didn't feel
safe?"*

I lost it. I sobbed and cried and yelped and heaved.
I lost control of my body. Now I see this was another panic
attack, a term I wouldn't become familiar with until
college, but something I struggled with for years by then.

There I was, given permission to be honest for once.

I said no.

If my answer was no, why was I crying? Why I was
emotional? They attempted to dig deeper. I just continued
to grieve in front of them. I mourned the last four years of
my life. I mourned the part of my life going forward that
would continue to conceal this shame in me.

When I composed myself, I asked to leave. The
dean said they had more questions. She told me my
reaction concerned her deeply. I turned to the principal
and said, "Haven't I been through enough? Please don't
make me do this. Don't make me do this to my family." I
said it with such clarity and focus, I don't know where the
power came from I didn't wait for a response. I closed the
yearbook in front of them and walked out of the office. It
was only 9:30 am, but I left school. I drove to the field
where our final debauchery took place, our final
rendezvous.

I parked my car, took off my school uniform and pulled on a sweatshirt and some running shorts. With no one in sight, I hopped on the top of my car and observed the surroundings. When I was fourteen, I told myself I'd never return there. I made a promise I'd never give that space my energy. In a sense, I never did. The fourteen-year-old me who was pillaged ceased to exist at some point. I reflect back on who I was and truly see her as a separate entity from the person I am now. Trying to understand the fundamental switch that happens upon being raped is harrowing, basically impossible. For four years, I ran, I dodged, I hid the truth. And I was successful in it. With only two weeks at that school left, I thought I made it. Had I made it those two final weeks, no one ever would have known about it, I can assure you of that.

Hours passed before I moved from my spot. It was a meditation of sorts, kneeled on top of my car. Thoughts ceased within me. Instead, I took stock of my body. This horrible, putrid body he decimated, but this body I further destroyed.

Even now, no matter the hours of therapy or the number of coping mechanisms I utilize, I will never exist outside of this trauma. There are days when I have to remind myself and convince myself that yes, I was raped. This sort of invasion completely warped my mind, forcing me to constantly second-guess myself. He'd tell me one thing, but I'd wonder if perhaps I was being manipulated into believing a half-truth of sorts. I have healed and grown, but it is foolish to think I will ever view sex as purely intoxicating. It is foolish to think I can ever look at this body of mine and erase from my memory the force of his tall, vapid, strong body pushing down on mine.

In writing this, I keep thinking, backspacing, and rewriting, because I'm acutely aware of what others will think of this. What is my brother going to think? It brings me immediately to tears when I consider what my family will think now that this part of me is published for anyone to see. I know now when I am googled, inevitably, someone can learn that I was raped. I choose to think of this in the same way that I view my eating disorder though.

I am not ashamed. Not anymore. I can't be. If I cower in the shame the world thrusts at me, I'm the one who loses. If I let shame mold into me, I then have to live my life confined to these chains I never asked for.

This is my story. I have to take ownership of it. Though I didn't choose for this to happen, it is part of my story and I can either drown or thrive as a result. I also need to acknowledge that just because this is my story to tell, it doesn't necessarily mean others will respond with grace and care.

It took over four years to admit I was raped to my best friend, and an additional two years to ever write about it. The first sentence I ever typed out only carried a portion of the truth, something along the lines of, "I was taken advantage of by an older man." That is too eloquent, as I read it now. There is no beautiful way to describe rape. He was well aware of the disgusting reality of his actions. His shoving, thrusting, and groping. Every breath was an act of violent hatred toward the innocence I quickly lost. He took from me what every young human deserves to have ownership over and left me subject to my indignity.

No one is ready to face the idea that many people are raped by someone they know. Others are quick to conceive of the hurdle in overcoming such trauma when it is a back-alley stranger masked by a dark gray hoodie and ill-fitting jeans. I'm sorry to say, that's not always the truth. We may always want to think the best of people, but when so many men and women are raped by their acquaintances, we cannot ignore this any longer.

No one wants to talk about rape. I get it. You think I want to write about it? You think I've enjoyed sitting here, drinking my tea, listening to Boccherini, while I write about a man I was supposed to trust forcing himself onto me while shouting utterances that haunt me every night? I sat for two weeks begging the wheels of mind to churn it out, so I could be done with this chapter. I wouldn't put it past people to skip over this chapter of my story. But you have to realize, this *is* my story. This is the defining chapter of my story. When I think of my life in terms of "before," and, "after," I don't think of it as pre-eating disorder and then recovery. I think of my life as "before I was raped," and the aftermath. Valentine 's Day of 2011 is the ultimate marker for my life irrevocably changing.

One of the most horrifying reasons why I never wanted to talk about the rape is because I believed it was my fault for the longest time. Did I say no? Did I push him off of me? Did I let it happen? Did I enjoy it? Did I give him the impression that I wanted it? I asked myself all of those questions, but I took too long (or so I believed) to find the answers. At that point, I assumed it was too late to tell someone. Now, I know it is never too late. But here I write this out so you can see that when someone is raped, and others wonder why they don't speak out, it's because the body fails them. Self-doubt consumes the mind. All I could ask myself was, *"What did I do wrong?"*

With sexual violence sordidly rampant in society today, I found it became much easier for everyone to forgive those in the spotlight. When was the last time you thought about Kevin Spacey? How many of you continued to watch House of Cards? My acquaintances did. Or what about Junot Diaz? His novels are still on college syllabi around the world. Louis C.K. is back on the stand-up grid, and he is having no trouble with ticket sales. Look at our president, Mr. Trump himself. Everyone is so quick to forget. Let me tell you something—no one who has been raped forgets, even for a day. It left me with a resounding hesitance to hug men. If someone even looks an ounce like him, I can't and will not touch them. In life, we all have choices to make and milestones to achieve. My rapist took a vital choice from me. Being raped shook my belief in humanity.

Snares, shame, and silence.

TIME PASSED. I DID NOT HEAL.

After what happened months before, God and I were on the outs; I had zero interest in changing that. Every day, I prayed, asking for absolvement of my sins, asking for guidance. When my prayers of forgiveness went unanswered, my prayers turned into questions. No, "Dear God." No, "Amen." My prayers were, "Why?" and, "Again?" and, "Am I okay?" It always came back to, "Why?" When that question was met with muted replies, I gave up on prayer entirely.

Then, I took to the Bible itself. Knowing that prayer was the automatic response to any trial in life, I reckoned perhaps this was too difficult a conversation to be had over a nightly prayer with God. To me, that made sense. I wanted to rationalize what happened. More than anything though, I wanted to find a way to make God respond to me. Living in a world where someone could take me and do what they wanted with me was far harder to bear if there was no higher entity watching over and protecting me.

Though I'd attended Christian schooling my entire life, I knew hardly anything about the actual content of the Bible. Little did I know there were actual testimonies of rape found in the Bible. When I came across the passages in 2 Samuel (2 Samuel 13:1-22, to be exact), I thought I found my shining light. The direct and specific answer I was looking for. The naive, poor, sad eyes of my fourteen-year-old self literally thought this story was planted in the Bible, just so I could have that very moment of taking it in and finding a way to heal.

Sitting on the floor of my childhood bedroom, back perched up against the railing of my bed frame, I scoured the text. I devoured it, first just implanting every word into my head, permanently cementing the letters down. I didn't read for analysis or retainment, I just needed to see the whole story for what it was, take in every bit of syntax, just to calm myself down. A story like mine exists. Just that revelation on its own gave me an inch of comfort. Bear in mind this was 2011, and I was fourteen years old. #MeToo was not a thing, and no one dared even speak about sex around someone my age in the community I grew up in.

I read the story once, then again. Then three more times. I didn't process anything. I burst into tears. Silent, hiccupping sobs, as I shushed myself, calming it away before anyone in my house heard me. Finally, I felt compelled to take in the story entirely.

Tamar. Daughter of King David, Israelite King. Often, people refer to Jesus as the son of David, speaking to royal origin. This is that same David. They fall under the same genealogy of Abraham as well, therefore Tamar, though female, has important blood running through her in Christian tradition. Tamar was a princess; in the first sentence of her mentioning, she is noted as beautiful. In the most widely accepted translations of the Bible, the word beautiful is written only nineteen times. This beauty enticed the likes of her half-brother Amnon, so much so, it turned into an obsession for him. Being that Tamar was then next described as a virgin (notice the remarkably pitiful adjectives women receive in the Bible?), Amnon appeared ill-fated. He couldn't do a single thing about it even if he wanted to.

And then he changed that.

Unable to get his mind off of her, Amnon and his "adviser," conjured up a plan to get Amnon and Tamar alone with one another, under the approval of King David himself.

Tamar, obeying orders from her father, went to visit her half-brother, who immediately propositioned the idea of lying together (biblical prose for having sex). She refused. Not only did she refuse, this woman who was not to be trifled with also called him out on it. "Don't force me!" She called the act, "wicked." Before it happened, she cried out asking him what would happen after; "where could I get rid of my disgrace?"

And then, you know what happens next? "But he refused to listen to her, and since he was stronger than she, he raped her."

Oh, fine reader, just you wait. The story is not over.

Immediately after finishing, Amnon looked at her with disgust. The Bible says he then loathed her with "an intense hatred." He called to his servant and had her thrown out on the street, where she accumulated ashes to cover herself with as a shroud of shame. She tore apart the robes she wore, as they were the cloth of virgins. Her father, King David, did nothing to protect her.

Reading this conclusion at fourteen years old, I sat there stupefied. I thought I found every answer I ever needed, but this only destroyed me. It confused me as well. Following this little aside (because that truly is what it is, being only twenty-two verses and then immediately shooting off to another story), I scanned the text, looking for the meaning, the lesson, the hope, the guidance. Instead, I was left with an arched forehead, blotchy skin, and no sense of resolution.

I didn't want to give up yet.

I read it again and again. Part of me wanted to bring it up to teachers, just on the chance they could provide clarity. But even the idea of that paralyzed me. This was no normal story. On what planet could I walk up to a teacher at my tiny private, Christian school, ask about this random story I found in a book of the Bible I'd never encountered before, ask for answers, and *not* have them give me the third degree? It was impossible, and there was no way I'd give myself over to revealing this part of me yet. The coach still worked at the school. He was very much involved in the campus. I wasn't ready. I decided to keep searching for answers on my own, reminding myself of all the rundown clichés.

"God works in mysterious ways."
"God has his own timing."
"Be still. Be patient."
"God has a plan."

I told myself these all day long. In fact, I became a more active and prominent Christian while in school. I paid attention more during chapel services, I participated in biblical discussions, and when a teacher asked for a volunteer to pray, I shot my hand right up before the request even finished its utterance.

Tamar's story existed in the Bible for thousands of years, and when I looked around, no one else was up in arms about it. I didn't realize it was because everyone chose not to address it. I told myself I wasn't a good enough Christian to understand the hidden meaning. I gestured it likely was a parable. The story wasn't about the rape itself but something deeper, something profound and ready to show me the unconditional love of the Lord. I searched and searched.

Within me, I knew there had to be more to the story. What I saw though, was a man uncomfortable with the idea of someone refusing him and taking power over the situation, resulting in a damaged woman. I wanted to see a story of boundless hope, but instead, I saw vile deception. I knew I had to be wrong. (Spoiler alert: I wasn't).

During this time, my Bible class learned the practice of biblical exegesis. Biblical exegesis is when a scholar dissects scripture based solely on the content. This form of interpretation branches out into several different methods, but I didn't learn of those until college. For freshmen in high school still following the scripted formats for essays where a question is an appropriate way to capture an audience, biblical exegesis was a lot simpler. For us, it meant simply taking a look at the story at hand and drawing out the intention of it existing in the Bible.

Before I move forward with this though, I need to say: writing a biblical exegesis as a fourteen-year-old in a private Christian school is *not* an indication of what a real biblical exegesis should look like. A real, true, credible biblical exegesis comes from authentic resources filled with quality research. Biblical exegesis is meant to give students of the Bible a means to mindfully grow in one's relationship with God. Secular exegesis (which was a lot of my collegiate work) comes from the same concept, just without the faith-based perspective of the author.

On the day that my teacher introduced this to us, I felt like I found my second chance at elucidation. This was how I could find the answers I needed. Though the assignment allowed us to choose any story in the Bible we wanted, I lacked the courage to set Tamar as my choice. Instead, I took on the task of doubling the work, doing one for school and one for myself. I gathered the tools from class and immersed myself in evenings of Googling biblical exegeses on Tamar, hoping to find something that resonated with the vacant, hollow within me.

Anticipation in me building this all up, knowing I was closer to understanding myself in this post-tragic state I struggled to place, I devoured article after article. Nothing helped. Hardly any essays addressed the rape itself. Hardly any of the biblical exegeses I came across took the time to address the story from a female perspective. Everything centered around Amnon's wickedness, his sin, his poor character.

I didn't find a single article speaking to Tamar's role in this story. Analyses and interpretations focused the insight on why Amnon was wicked. Actually, several articles discuss the "obvious" (in their words) claim that Amnon was overwhelmed by genuine love for Tamar. They were only half-siblings after all. An assumption like that made no difference to me because even then, naive as I was, I knew there was no love in that act.

My search led me to several conclusions, nothing of hope: "trust no one" and "rape is shameful." That must be why everyone shuns the story of Tamar. No one wants to take the time to discuss how one heals from such trauma, therefore it must be something to feel shame for. That was the logic I fell into. Suppressing the story was easier than addressing it, I told myself. After all, the church does take the time to travel through stories of murder, deceit, and pillaging thousands. The only rational conclusion I was able to come with was that rape was worse than all of this. If my teachers could stand up before me and talk about people invading other villages and slaughtering thousands of men in the name of God, but they couldn't talk about a woman having her virginity stripped from her, I was damned. That's what I really and truly thought. I concluded I was condemned and forever forgotten in the eyes of God.

As my search deepened, I came across a few exegeses that all shared one interesting perspective. "Beauty is a snare to many; it was so to her." I didn't even need to look that article back up. I'm sure if you type into Google something along the lines of "Tamar biblical exegesis," and search for that quote, that exact verbiage would come up. I read that when I was fourteen, hidden away in my bedroom, and I have never forgotten that. It was the closest I ever came to finding my answers. I wasn't satisfied, but that was something.

Eventually, my energy to research this all feigned. There was only so much a fourteen-year-old could do with twenty-two verses and hardly any exegesis that actually addressed the rape aspect of the story.

I never considered myself beautiful. I don't think I ever thought of myself as the opposite either, though; it just wasn't on my mind. Life back then encompassed gymnastics, friends, and school. I loved school. I didn't spend time thinking about whether or not I was beautiful. Then, I read that line. *"Beauty is a snare to many; it was so to her."* I read that same sentiment shared by other online pastors in a pattern of synonyms. It stuck with me.

One day, on my way home from school, I sat next to my brother as he drove me home. With the school year coming to an end, the finality of these car rides weighed on us both, knowing that next year he'd be at university. A Day to Remember blasted through the stereo as we rolled down the windows attempting to break ourselves from some of the heat. I turned to him, a bit loudly to be heard over the music, and told him I had a question for him.

He muted the music, ready to listen. "Do you think I am beautiful?" I paused. "Not as my brother, but just as another human being. What do you think?"

I don't know what in me prompted the question— to him of all people, at that moment, but it came out, and I couldn't take it back. He glanced over at me and laughed, "Of course you are. I mean, that's a weird question to ask me, but yes, Julia, you are beautiful. My friends say it all the time."

"Really?" I asked.

"Yeah."

"When you say friends, do you mean your guy friends or your female friends?"

"Do you think my guy friends would tell me they think my little sister is cute?" He replied, and I could audibly hear that eye roll.

"Right. Ok, thank you."

"Sure, bud."

In the final thoughts of the biblical story, there is one final remark from Tamar's other brother who, in comfort, tells her in the aftermath, "Be quiet. Don't take this thing to heart."

So, that's what I did. I learned to shut up and play my role.

I continued my image of excelling in Bible class, memorizing weekly verses, writing eloquent reflections on how these moments of scripture play out in my life. No one was the wiser. The months following my rape were a formative period of time in which I understood what it meant to take on a clandestine persona, to curate a life of hidden secrets, with no one suspecting otherwise. I replaced authenticity with approval, knowing that would get me farther in the real world.

The Second Event

WHAT I AM ABOUT TO SHARE is a defining moment in my life, on par with the sexual assaults I experienced months before this event. This is the time in my life that clearly divides my memories into "before" and "after." This is tragedy. Even so, I question putting this all into words. This is not my story to share, but it set me on my course for the rest of my life.

I think about this moment, this memory, this tragedy every day. I live my life navigating the world with this event almost always hovering in the background, the distilled decanter of my mind. For me, I cannot tell the honest truth without the gore, the gruesome details. I witnessed a death that should never have happened only yards away from me. But at the same time, to know someone who loved this girl would read this is more than enough for me to gloss over those details. She and her family are the ones who get to tell this story. I, on the other hand, was simply a bystander. I've done a lot of healing in my life, but this is one area of my mind I have made little progress in healing, if only because I don't feel worthy of it. I feel more shame for how I reacted to this event than I do for anything else in my life.

I question putting it here, but I know I have to. If I'm going to write the honest truth, the honest depiction of how cruel mental illness can be, I had to find the courage to write two main events in my life. This is the second. For me, I want to pay respect to everyone involved, but I also have to find the balance of explaining the gruesome details.

This story is not about me, and I made it about me. In a way, I still make it about me. I don't know how to shut that off. Of course, I know it is about other people, people who are so much worse off; they lost their sister, daughter, best friend. I lost a friend, but I did not have it as bad as anyone else involved. I was the one to get off easy, and that has left with me with so much guilt.

Part of achieving the perfect young Christian girl archetype I set my sights on included regularly attending church. This is not something I ever excelled at. One or two times every year, a friend invited me to his congregation or youth group and I'd actually take him up on his offer. One summer evening only months after my assaults, I sat on the edge of my friend's pool, swaying my toes around, dipped into the side of the cool water, creating mini tornadoes in the plunging waves below me, when I was asked to stay a little bit longer. He asked me to enjoy dinner with his family and come see the youth group. Usually, a request like this was met with a polite no from me, as I'd much rather have gone home to watch television and be on my own.

When he mentioned I already knew several of the kids in youth group from school, I realized this was actually a night I might enjoy instead of feeling like I needed to impress strangers. Minimal energy required of me, I said yes. Considering I was already with the people who'd take me to church, it was an easy way to find myself back in the fold of acceptable Christian behavior, something I'd lacked in since February.

Out on the back patio, we let our bodies soak in the heat of the setting sun, munching on a freshly cooked pan of frozen pizza. I alternated between sips of coke and messy bites filled with dripping sauce and slightly burnt pepperoni. The sharp crunch satisfied my hunger after an active day out in the sun. The conversation around me put me at ease. As I observed the family, I saw this was not a formal church gathering we were about to set off to, but rather a communal gathering of fellowship and union while worshipping God. Once finally dry from the pool, my friend and his family changed into jeans, tank tops, and flip-flops, or something of the like. The air around me felt unaffectedly welcoming, further convincing me to give the youth group a chance.

As much as I would like to tell a story about how the message overwhelmed me with the presence of God's love, that's not why this particular night is written here. I didn't find myself desperate to redeem myself in the eyes of the Lord. The sermon (if one could call a twenty-something man with shaggy hair, ripped jeans, and a Plain White T's t-shirt sitting on a bean bag chair in front of thirty teenage kids a sermon) centered around the idea of walls. All around us we construct walls, building boundaries and barriers, protecting ourselves from elements of the world we fear. Because of Jesus, our walls are able to come down. He destroys our walls, if we allow him, bringing us closer to God. To further prove his point, the youth pastor smashed a Jenga wall, spilling logs all around the room. This was met with giggles—always a sign of an effective sermon for teenagers. I stood there alongside friends singing worship songs while also staring at the clock.

This is not the story of me finding my religion. This is the story that keeps me up at night.

At the end of the night, several of us lounged on large bean bag chairs, snacking on goldfish and exchanging summer plans. I found myself in conversation with a friend from school. I always admired her, but more so from afar. We shared classes together and definitely had our fair share of laughter and memories with one another. Not a best friend, but a good friend. She encompassed a lot of what I hoped for myself as a female trying to make it in this world. This girl was smart, studious, cheerful, athletic—likely to go on and play soccer collegiately—and admired by many around her. If one had the ability to turn handwriting into computer font, people would purchase her typography the minute it came onto the market. Her cheeky sense of humor was always playful, and while her jokes didn't always hit, she made you smile for trying.

Much of this night is a blur, but I do remember select portions of our conversation. As others moved outside to the playground next to the church, we found ourselves alone in the large, dimly lit room. She peered around, scoping out hidden eavesdroppers and leaned in to me. I mimicked her move, closing the space between us. With a keen look in her eye, she said to me, "I wish you and I were closer."

I looked at her with such a question on my face and blurted out, "Why?" Realizing that might sound offensive after such a gracious confession, I then quickly qualified that by telling her how much I'd enjoy that, but I also didn't understand. My self-worth had quickly dropped in the previous months. I couldn't fathom how someone wanted to build a stronger friendship with me back then. I didn't even understand how I still had the friends from before.

Clear as day, she looked at me with such sad bewilderment. If I were an artist, I'd draw her face in this way every single day. She replied, "You make people happy. There's a light about you."

I remember thinking how grateful I was for the poor lighting because my eyes welled up in tears. If I ever had to describe this girl before she said that to me, the first word out my mouth would have been "sunny." She always was so ebullient, so bright. For her to tell me I was a light astounded me. I thanked her for her kindness. She encouraged me to return to youth group the following week. I gave her a promise of, "I'll try," knowing I'd likely not, but I wanted nothing to sour that moment between us.

Nearing the end of the evening, we headed outside slowly joining the other in saying goodbyes and gather up the carpool groups. I found myself in conversation with two older girls I'd never met before, talking about nonsense. It was a nice warm evening, one of which meant for late night strolls and midnight ice cream. The parking lot stood aglow under overhead stadium lights, giving everyone the soft yellow glint reminiscent of sunset reflection. It was a large lot, with cars everywhere. This parking lot lay up against the Tujunga wash. Tujunga wash acts as a tributary for the Los Angeles River. Its purpose is mainly flood control, but considering Los Angeles averages less than fifteen inches of rain a year, most often the wash is dry. The wash is eighteen feet deep and nothing to fool around with.

In the midst of my conversation with these strangers, headlights on a car turned on, diverting all of our attention over to the other side of the parking lot. I noticed it was the car I was supposed to hitch a ride from. Then, the reverse lights came on. Knowing I was supposed to be in that car, I realized I likely had kept my friends waiting. My friend graciously offered to take me home even though I lived far away from everyone else. I started jogging toward the car, hoping to make it less of a wait than what they expected. I stared at those reverse lights as I witnessed the most horrific tragedy take place in front of me.

The car reversed far too quickly. It jutted backward, as though the car had something wrong with it. The brakes slammed as it turned the corner. Then, it jutted back again, falling backward over the fence and falling into the wash sideways, with the driver's side hitting the concrete floor.

All I remember is the car's alarm going off and the horn being in a constant state of honking. It didn't let up. I heard loud screaming. Shrieking. Bloody murder of yelping and pleading for help. I was the closest person to the scene, and the first person to look over. I don't even know if I could describe what I saw for the book because it was so horrific. I've written about it for years in journals because it is all I see in my nightmares, but I don't want it here. The blood, the lifeless body.

Instinctively, though all I saw were her limbs, I knew who was in the car. It was the friend from only a half hour before, telling me she wanted to build a stronger friendship with me. Before I was able to process anything, I called 911. My other good friend, along with everyone in the youth group sprinted over only strides behind. The other person in the car continued to scream, while we all did what we could to help. Several people also called 911, and a few people climbed down into the wash. I sat on the edge of the wash, usually barricaded by a fence but now exposed. For the first time in months, I clasped my hands together, kept my eyes open though, and prayed in such a way that I believed there was something on the other end of my thoughts listening. I didn't realize, but I'd missed that component for a long time.

Words were lost on me in this prayer. For all of religious history, the idea of mysticism and speaking in tongues has existed as controversial, but in this moment, I think I came pretty close to it. I knew in such a tragic moment, where everything looked desolate, words would never suffice the sheer "please" within me to keep this girl alive. I prayed in emotions and wishes, not words.

Though only nine minutes later, the impatience of waiting finally brought ambulances and fire trucks. They took care of it all, whisking everyone away to the hospital, shooing us all from the scene so they could execute their jobs properly. All around me I saw people in hysterics, uncontrollably crying and sobbing. I didn't shed a tear; not because I didn't care, not in the slightest. I was in such a state of shock. I felt vacant. I saw decay and disruption and death looming, but everything about the scene felt misplaced. I knew it wasn't supposed to happen to her. Not to that beautiful, inspiring girl.

I lost a dear friend far before her time was supposed to end. She had so much in her life to live for, and there I was—a vile creature.

For a very long time, a very long time, I used to pray to go back in time so God could replace her with myself. Constantly, I replayed the night over and over in my head, wondering what I could have done differently to save her. If we'd talked longer, or perhaps had we not talked at all. Or, even, maybe if I hadn't even come that night, she might still be alive. I beckoned with my mind, trying to find some way in which it was both my fault and how I could have prevented it. I couldn't bear the thought of this beautiful soul no longer existing, especially when I still did.

I really believed the wrong person was taken that night. She was *never* supposed to be in that car that night. That was not the car meant to take her home. That was the car meant to take me home. I remember staring up at the sky after I could no longer bear to look at the accident below me, and all of a sudden, it was as though a heavy weight fell onto me. Somewhat like a shroud; that's the best way I can describe it. It covered me, giving the dark blue night sky an eerie green glow to it. In those few seconds, I understood completely. God took the wrong girl that night. I wasn't under the impression that God made mistakes, but I knew that God took the wrong girl that night. After the shame I'd brought, of course, it was me who was meant to die, not this innocent girl with so much hope for the future. She'd not soiled her body. This girl had ambition and a true heart for God. No one had to plead with her to attend church. Her life would have been filled with abundance and longing to do God's will. There I was sitting through a church service watching the seconds tick on by. I wallowed under the pressure of that shroud, feeling heavier than ever, and knowing I deserved that, but I deserved so much more penance.

I have a very hard time experiencing anything good in life without feeling tremendous guilt. I get to fall in love, but she doesn't. I potentially will have a family of my own one day; she will not. That is really hard for me. Very, very hard. Because of this, because I was incapable of truly processing this, I vowed to spend the whole of my life punishing myself in whatever ways I was able to drum up. I didn't know what that meant at the time, but it didn't take long for me to uncover.

The aftermath of the accident brought about an amazing sense of community. I witnessed an entire school and congregation come together to support the families affected. Memorials held, candle lighting inflamed, songs sung, testimonies shared. People who hardly spoke to one another collapsed into each other's arms, reminding one another how precious each life is. I saw people take time to really listen to others. I saw people pray earnestly, rather than lightly fold their eyelids shut waiting to perk up when they heard the concluding syllables, amen. Many occasions passed in which I could have and should have participated, taking the time to grieve and mourn. But I didn't. I wasn't ready for it. I stood by and watched, observing people love on one another, wondering what that level of vulnerability felt like.

In all of that, that beautiful decay. I felt lost and alone. Every night, I deplored the idea of sleep because when my body did give way to the need for slumber, I was met with the sheer terror of feeling the visceral physicality of the accident. Every night brought the nightmare of either of being in the car or watching the car from my point of view, all over again. Sometimes I was her. Sometimes I was another passenger in the car. Sometimes I was myself. I always got it wrong. Regardless of the night terror, I was always in the wrong. Some nights I drowned in the blood, caught in the ringlets of her saturated, bloody hair. I'd wake up screaming, covered in sweat, crying out, *"why, why, why?!"* Not *"why does this dream keep happening?"* but, *"why wasn't it me?"*

This moment in the lives of everyone who bore witness to it has nothing to do with me. This story is not about me. It shouldn't be about me. I, out of everyone, suffered the least. Sure I witnessed it, but she wasn't my child. She wasn't my best friend. She was a friend, but she was not my life. She was someone I cared for, but I did not suffer the burden of grieving her death as much as her family. Her death is not about me.

Even as I knew this, I couldn't stop thinking about how I was affected by it all. I knew her death was not about me, and yet I was haunted by it all. This story paints me in a bad light, and it should. I was so selfish during this time. I know it, and I want you who are reading it to think of me as selfish during this time. There is no other way to see it than for exactly this. I made a tragedy that had nothing to do with me all about me.

During the time, I felt very alone and also very muted. No one ever asked if I was okay, and rightfully so. I was not the person to worry about in this instant. I was not the person people needed to focus on. I was healthy, yards away from the car. Sure. I witnessed a tragedy, but I *witnessed* it. I lived, so I should have nothing to complain about. That is absolutely right; I believe that wholeheartedly. I am not the point of that tragedy. I am at the corner of the story, hidden behind a flipped tab because in those moments, in those months of grieving, I didn't matter.

I know that. It's difficult for me to talk about this because, for me, I feel like I should never seek out consolation for enduring what I did. It was nothing in comparison to what others felt. For me though. I really struggled with what happened because I really was traumatized by that. Being traumatized by things nowadays are so often a term of mockery, or it's issued too lightly, but I honestly was traumatized. I learned what it meant to be traumatized by what happened.

Time drew on and people around me healed. I saw the conversation about the accident dwindle and come to restorative ends. People clung onto each other in a new and deeper way, but one of which no longer required mentioning of the accident. By the time school rolled around the following year, there were football games and homework and other ideas to occupy the minds of my peers. I followed suit, knowing that now was too late to bring up my own unresolved feelings about it all. My night terrors didn't stop. My lack of sleep suppressed my mind, making me less inclined to interact with my friends. Any brain power I had, I reserved for my school work. Isolation was my solace. I didn't need to expend extra energy on fulfilling my friendships; therefore, it was easier to keep my secrets.

"Be quiet. Don't take this thing to heart."

Any time something good happened to me after that, whether it be a high mark on a test or an award, her face popped into my mind. Then, my coach's face followed. When I saw her, I only felt guilt. When I saw him, I knew I didn't deserve anything that happened to me, anything I earned. He made me feel as though anything I received was in jest, only because I'd deceived everyone around me. And he was right. Everything I did was a show, an act I put on because I was too terrified to tell people what was going on in my heart and mind. I knew it was murky, nothing of the standard for someone who should and would excel in life.

Any time I felt compelled to burst out in anger or in grief, I remembered those words. They held power over me. I felt cold and departed from God, but the Bible was the Bible, and I knew its authority, whether I felt inclined to trust God was listening to me or not. As the Bible declared, I learned to quiet myself, express gratitude that I was still alive, and continue to press on, hoping to make myself into a Christian worthy of forgiveness for all of the horridness I'd caused in the world.

Silence never got me into trouble. Though it wasn't the answer I'd hope the Bible would provide, it allowed me to slide by and go unnoticed. I liked that a whole lot better than people finding out my secrets.

The year taught me two things: silence is good; beauty is dangerous.

The promise of a subtle escape.

THAT NEXT YEAR BROUGHT ABOUT MANY changes; one of which being the decision to quit gymnastics. Lots of reasons led up to this moment. While I knew it was the right decision, knowing that did not make it any easier.

I felt lost after I quit gymnastics. People at school knew me as "Julia the gymnast." That was literally my email growing up. It was everything to me. It was special, thereby defining me, giving me an air of eminence.

Having said goodbye to the sport, I became just Julia. I did not like being "*just Julia*." I needed something to fill that gaping hole in my heart, and I hunted for something to fill the void. At the time, cheerleading tryouts had just been announced, taking place the following week.

Cheerleading. I didn't know what to think of the sport. I didn't know what to think of the girls on the team, and I worried about whether or not they'd like me, or if I'd fit in. I just wanted to fall into step somewhere, go unnoticed. After little encouragement, I gave it a shot. It came rather easy, in the sense that I was familiar with learning routines and tumbling. By no means was I a good cheerleader, but I liked the performing aspect. I liked it all well enough. I made it work by building friendships with the other girls on the team.

During those first few months acclimating to the team, a new confidence surged in me, leading me to understand that putting on a show for others, in turn, puts on a show for myself. It became the easiest, most alluring facade for me. I loved knowing how to turn myself "*on*," always aware that people could never know how my day actually went. As long as I stood in front of a crowd and smiled away, waving my arms, no one would know the truth. This, I confused with confidence. It didn't matter. To me, it just made sense.

As I look back on my high school experience, I am both surprised and pleased to say these are the friendships during that time in which the girls had the best relationships with food. These are the girls that would gorge on Taco Bell in between football games, stay out late for chocolate milkshakes and french fries, spooning off each other's whipped cream. Together, we baked cookies late into the nights of slumber parties, always fueling our workouts with good, sustainable meals as well. In them, I saw not only balance, but fun. We worked hard in practice, but we always enjoyed ourselves as well.

When cheer practice started, I realized how wrong I was about cheerleaders. During tryouts, I was under the impression I'd have it easy. Arrogantly, I thought I'd sail right through cheer practice, but by the end of the first day, I realized my assumptions were unsound. The workouts provided by my cheerleading coaches were the most grueling I ever endured, but I loved feeling stronger.

At the same time, my body continued to transition from a child to a more womanly figure. Without effort on my end, I slimmed down a considerable amount. Though I was not in the practice of weighing myself, just a mere glance at an older picture was enough for me to see the difference. This, combined with my coaches giving us simple nutritional transitions made me develop a changed physique. Still not necessarily slim, but noticeably smaller. I trimmed down to a stockier, athletic version of my former body. Curves started to sort out on different parts of my body as well. As I looked in the mirror, I saw glimpses of what I'd look like as a fully formed woman. I liked what I saw.

Halfway through my first season as a cheerleader, I visited my doctor for my annual exam where I was informed I'd lost almost ten pounds. Sitting with my mom, I felt a wave of questioning pride. My mom looked over at me as she beamed and nodded her head in approval. I shrugged my shoulders and waved it off, though the thrill of that lower number gave me a new sense of satisfaction. I hadn't tried to lose that weight. I'd made easy changes that made no impact on my daily life. As we drove home, I remember considering what a difference I could make if I put in actual effort. That night, I started researching simple weight loss efforts and began my research into calorie counting and exercise regimens. None of this took significant hold on me, though. Not quite yet.

The next school year brought with it a season of immense change. Everything about my personality morphed. I don't know if others around me sensed it, though I'm sure my parents were well aware. If they did, they likely chalked it up to puberty or the natural progression of a young girl maturing and going through stages of sorting out personality defects. My gregarious spirit slowly dissipated, and I immersed myself into every activity that kept me busy. I started advanced placement courses, I stuck with cheerleading only, and I hung out on my laptop a whole lot more.

I signed up for Tumblr, an online platform where I first found myself introduced to blogging, though Tumblr is that only on a micro-scale. With many different methods of utilizing the site, teenagers including myself mainly used it to repost images within that blogger's set aesthetic. Initially, I re-posted poetry, landscapes, and cute animals, on par with just about every other teenage girl. Still gripping onto the romantic within me, this was another way to day dream, a moment to escape with every picture captured.

Tumblr, as opposed to Twitter and Instagram, always gave off an aura of privacy. It was not an account others were to know about, therefore the ability to write in more vulnerable forms was encouraged. I found myself typing out blurbs of hurt and sorrow. For anyone outside of me to read them, they hadn't the faintest idea what I referred to, but it gave me the sense of unburdening. It lightened my load, just a little bit. No one had to know what I meant, but also, I no longer had to keep maneuvering around the chaos in my head. It didn't erase everything, but it served as somewhat of a healthy coping mechanism.

In the abyss I created for myself, I found little to smile about, but I sourced out the fake energy I'd learned from cheerleading in all aspects of life. I worked hard to ensure no one around me knew the truth about the memories constantly flashing back in my head, perturbing every thought.

Again, due for my annual physical exam, my mom and I sat side by side in the car, humming along to an old Shania Twain CD, not having any particular feelings toward the appointment itself, just knowing it was a chore to check off the list.

I clocked in at another six pounds lost throughout the year, to which both my mom and the doctor gave me a mirrored nod of approval, just as the year before. This year though, rather than return their glee with a blank face, I joined them in the quiet excitement. Not one of us made more than a small note of gratification, but we all could feel it in the air; I was doing something right. I was making myself "more." I was making myself attractive. The doctor herself told me I looked beautiful. Not healthy. She told me I looked beautiful.

On the way home, my mom mentioned I should take a glance at pictures from a year before. I told her I didn't think there would be much of a difference, but she said it was worth looking into. Sure enough, I saw how much I'd changed. The doctor was right, I remember thinking to myself. Conventionally, I was much more beautiful. Chubby cheeks no longer overwhelmed my face, and I had a much more socially acceptable body. I felt like I was looking at a "before" picture of myself.

That night, I went onto Tumblr and searched "before and after" pictures of others, wanting to see the progress others made toward health. Then, I found a different side of Tumblr. It was the most sudden thing. As I learned the social media platform, I saw there were accounts dedicated to healthy living and losing weight. Intrigued, I subscribed to a few of the accounts. Rather than posting images of pink sunsets and husky puppies, these accounts portrayed images of thigh gaps, exercise plans, and low-calorie meal ideas. "Before and after pictures" came by the plenty, and something within me grasped onto that.

I created a new Tumblr account, signing up under an anonymous URL where I created a "fitblr," someone who belonged to the fitness aesthetic of Tumblr. I spent all of my free time scrolling, browsing healthy recipes, exploring different exercise regimens, researching and memorizing calories counts. It began slow. I did not calorie count initially. I just ate healthier. I became mindful of the food I ate, and seemingly overnight, I felt like a new person. I start a new exercise program, and it kicked my butt. Additionally, I started running.

My entire life, I despised running. I used to be the girl who faked painful period symptoms on the mile-run day in middle school PE class.

It wasn't the idea of looking thinner and therefore more beautiful that played a role. As a teenage that inevitably plays somewhat of a role, but my mind shut that portion off before it began. It was the act of the transformation; of taking control of one's life and showing others the sheer will and determination of such an evolution. I realized how much I craved that. So much of what happened in the past two years happened because of things outside of my control. If I soaked into this challenge, I could finally have something happen because I chose for it to, and not because I was forced into dealing with something.

I followed everything and anything. I learned what a calorie was and how many a female "should" eat. I downloaded My Fitness Pal. My descent began.

It was slow at first. If anything, weight loss for me had no ill intentions. It was all for the pursuit of health and owning my body. I worked out only very lightly, and it varied in the type of exercise. I didn't hold any rules or restrictions for myself. I simply explored. I had fun. I tried new recipes, and I learned what made my body feel good. I even took up running, which I'd loathed for my entire life. I learned how fulfilling it felt to challenge and fuel my body.

Nothing about it became unhealthy until others took notice. When it was just in my head, I felt self-validated. I didn't need others to approve of my behavior. It just felt fun to finally have something fill my mind rather than the constant criticism and haunting memories of what happened before. But when others started to take notice, I sought so much value in their compliments. After feeling so unworthy for so long, I took to any bit of validation. I sourced my energy in it, knowing it was fleeting, knowing I may never get another chance to feel that treasured. People admired me, told me I inspired them to eat healthier. I distinctly remember a teacher remarking on my radiance. I looked radiant. No one ever paid that much attention to me as they did in those initial few months of trying to be healthier.

This is where I struggle to accurately describe what it was like for me, because it never had a single modicum of meaning for me to become more beautiful in the eyes of others. That's not what I wanted at all. Losing weight allowed me to tap into a part of my mind that shut off everything else. When I ran, a wave of calm washed over me. It cleared my thoughts. Running acted as a mental silence. It then manifested into my physical disappearance, but initially, it only was meant to quiet the voices within me. Growing stronger gave me the comfort of knowing that maybe next time, I could protect myself. Eating better gave me the mental clarity to excel in my courses.

I couldn't tell you the exact moment it switched over, but it did seem almost immediate. When I first set out on this health spurt, I had intentions of weighing a certain number. The day I hit that made me feel more successful than any grade I ever received, any accomplishment in gymnastics, any genuine compliment about my personality. That number was the sole indicator of my worth at that moment. I felt invincible. I stared at myself for nearly an hour in the mirror. Being a teenage girl, I clearly did not have any pressing matters to attend to that I had the luxury of just hanging out in the mirror and staring at myself. I saw nothing wrong with it. (This sounds awful now.) I lauded over myself. I took pictures.

A while later, my family woke up, and I heard the clanging of breakfast bowls in the kitchen. I looked at the clock; I'd been up for three hours. I already exercised. I wasn't hungry. The satisfaction of my weight dropping to my goal was enough to fill me. I didn't have breakfast that day. I noticed how easy it was to skip the meal. Lunch was only a few hours away, and my mind occupied itself with scrolling through Tumblr, looking at the bodies of models who I now resembled in terms of weight.

The problem was, once I hit the goal weight, I changed nothing about my daily routine. I continued to plummet in weight. I hadn't upped my caloric intake. I didn't reduce my exercise regime. If anything, I sharpened it, fine-tuned it, ensured I always did exactly what I did to get me to my goal weight. I tightened the reins because I was so scared to lose that feeling of success. This was the first thing in my life that properly took me out of thinking about my failures. I had no sense for the outside world. It was all me, me, me. I was so awful.

The more research I did, the worse it got. Read an article claiming a vegetarian diet promotes weight loss? Done. I became a vegetarian. While I claimed my vegetarianism out of ethical reasons, I knew all along it was a ruse. I had no care for the animals. My priority was losing weight and losing weight only. Watch an interview defaming any and all sodas? The next day I declared I would drink only water and tea. As I dived deeper, my disorder intensified, though I made a strong claim of ignorance for an extended amount of time.

The denial of my own hunger was the source of my happiness. Declaring, "I'm not hungry," or convincing others I'd already eaten and having those statements work was the best accomplishment. It purveyed over everything else I could have done with my day. Soon enough, the act of consciously thinking through the various excuses I had at hand required no thought but instead was my automatic response. It was my default to deny myself nourishment.

I gulped water voraciously, chewed my way through a pack of gum every two or three days, filling the void of my hollow stomach. Fidgeting took over as a behavior I mindlessly relied on to burn calories throughout the hours I found myself confined to a chair at school. Everywhere I went, I insisted on walking, passing judgments on my family for opting for closer parking spots. "It doesn't hurt to walk a few extra steps."

Though I'd always claim my intentions were to help others around me, I demonized people's food choices quite a bit. If others grabbed a burger, I had to have a salad. If they had a salad with cheese on it, mine came without it. I always had to one-up others, needing to know I won. Everyone around me was losing a game that only I knew we were playing.

My daily routine included a running a mile in the morning, two hours of cheer practice, and also an hour and a half of musical rehearsal. I gave myself no break during this time. Food fell to the wayside, snacking on fruit throughout the day when I could remember to do so.

One of the faults of diet culture is that society is fixated specifically on weight loss. There are products and guides and plans that teach us how to lose weight. No one tells us how to maintain that healthy weight once it is reached though. I did not know what to do. I didn't know how to build my calories back up to a maintenance level. All I knew was that I felt good living off that lower caloric amount, and I had enough energy to continue this excessive amount of exercise I was doing. As a result, I changed nothing, knowing I felt good about that decision.

Stepping on the scale turned from a monthly habit to an almost daily task in my routine. Every time I stepped on, I saw a smaller number. And every time, I stepped off with a contented smile on my face. My confidence soared.

As my junior year came to a close, my school sent a large group of students on a mission trip during spring break. Out of my comfort zone and fed meals I had no control over, I realized for the first time how much my meals controlled my life. When I was in school, inundated with homework and various practices and rehearsals, I didn't have the time to ponder on the change my food mentality brought with it. There, in a cold, unstable tent, I sat there awake at night on the dusty ground in my sleeping bag, tallying up numbers. I brought with me a new journal, hoping to find profound spiritual reflection that would help me heal. Instead, I covered that notebook with various calorie counts as I estimated meals, hoping I'd stay under my self-prescribed calorie counts. I utilized my vegetarian label at the time to swerve meals. I ate hardly anything during the trip, and though I tried not to think about it, I know everyone around me started to see the truth, just as I did. Still, no one said anything.

One week later, when my parents picked me up from the school bus, I saw a glassy look in my dad's eyes. He told me I looked very thin. I shrugged my shoulders and told him the food wasn't good. I made some horribly inventive remark about not trusting food from "over there," (ugh, I know. I'm sorry) and let him know I was going to eat a lot in the coming days to make up for it. My dad quickly backtracked saying I looked good, and I repressed a smile. I loved hearing that. I loved hearing that so much.

One of my best friends asked me to prom, and all I could think about was shopping for another formal gown. My memories sent me straight back to the eighth grade. I did not feel prepared for it, but then again, I thought about all the weight I'd lost. "This time, I am different," I remember telling myself, psyching myself up for the occasion.

My parents wanted to come with me to try on dresses. They took me out for lunch, where I ate an actual substantial meal; a cheeseburger. The first one I'd eaten in over a year. I could tell my parents were watching me, ensuring I was eating. I didn't want to fight it. Not at that point. I knew I'd lost a lot of weight when I was away for the week, and I knew if I ate a little bit more for a few days, they'd lay off me, let it pass by. I devoured that cheeseburger, as though I reverted back to every basic primal instinct within me. I had to force myself back from ravishing it, knowing I'd need to savor it. I didn't think I'd let myself have another one for a very long time. Though they said nothing, my parents were impressed, nerves calmed.

As we drove over to the mall, I rubbed my chest. I picked the habit up years before as a way to quiet my anxiety. I don't know why I picked it up or where I saw someone do this, but it has always quieted voices in my head. Stroking my chest, a new sensation hit me. There was a bump of sorts. I rubbed harder and then slower, trying to understand what it was. I looked around at the world, as though the answer would appear in front of me. We pulled into a spot at the mall. As the engine shut off, I placed my hands by my side, avoiding any questions of my actions before I knew myself what I'd discovered.

Strolling through the different aisles, several gowns caught my eye. We pulled what I thought would have been the appropriate size for me and embarked on trying everything on. Shown to the fitting room by a less-than-enthused teenager working a job she couldn't care less about, I took the few moments of solace to look at myself in the mirror, hoping to discover what this newfound bump on my chest was. I didn't even need to step closer to the mirror to uncover what it was. As soon as I stripped down to my underwear, I glanced at myself and saw what it was. Bones. My bones were protruded out; not enough to cause any concern, but I'd never seen myself in that light.

I shifted to the side and glanced at the profile of this new body I owned. Flat and slim. I loved it. I looked back to the bones and grew nervous, not because I didn't like the look of it, but because I didn't want my parents to say anything.

Shifting my gaze toward the rack of gowns, I saw the majority of them were strapless. I slipped into one. Bones. It was the first thing I saw. I knew it was the first thing they would say.

"Are you doing ok?" my mom asked.

"Yes," I replied, looking at myself in the dress. I arched my back, contorting my elbows to zip it up, and I saw how loose the gown was. I checked the size: 0. Never in my life had I ever been remotely close to that size, and I didn't think I was close to that then. It made me smile. I was disappearing. The dress hung loosely on me, and though the words "anorexic" or "eating disorder" never properly entered my mind, I knew my parents would be concerned. Finally, my parents egged me out, but I covered my chest as they evaluated the gown.

"Well," my dad started, "what do you think?"

The gown was everything I ever could have wanted. A deep emerald green satin gown with embroidered lace appliques perfectly scattered, cascading down the silhouette. It was a gown I'd always envisioned wearing, but always still fearful of the confidence I utterly lacked. Cut in a deep sweetheart, I neither had the bust line nor a meager bit of fat on my body to suit the dress. All I saw were the prominent chest bones stuck out for all to see. I held back tears as I saw a gown I'd have to give up because I was never meant for something so beautiful.

"I don't like strapless, I don't think," I murmured, giving off an air of disgust toward the dress. Talking myself out of the dress as much as I was talking them out of it too. "I just don't feel comfortable."

"Can we see?" My mom asked, practically opening the door to the fitting room herself.

Knowing I had to give her something to see, I stepped out but wrapped my arms around my neck, both in a look of discomfort but also as a tool to conceal my deterioration. My mom shot me such a questioning look.

"You *don't* like this?"

"I think you look beautiful," my dad said.

With eyes locked on the floor, I shook my head.

"It's too much. It's not what I'm going for." I took a few steps back, already making my way to the fitting room.

"Well, alright," my mom replied, clearly disappointed.

I shuffled through a few other gowns in the fitting room, knowing each and every single one, if shown to my parents, would give off a rise of concern. Avoiding that, I pulled one with a high neckline. Intrigued by the royal blue, also satin like the first one, I slipped it on. Perfect. The high neckline concealed everything I needed to hide, and the a-line silhouette of the bottom flowed away from my figure. No one would need to see anything they didn't need to, and I still looked decent enough.

When I showed my parents, they both agreed. They liked it a lot. I don't know if they said this out of veracity or if because they could read me and saw this was the first gown I seemed somewhat comfortable in. They didn't ask questions. I seemed happy and that was the gown we went with. I felt confident this gown would not cause anyone to question me.

Turns out I was wrong.

The day of prom, my anxiety was at an all-time high. I had no control over the dinner meal, but all I knew was that it was pasta. I ran around during the day accomplishing various errands. I didn't eat anything up until the meal at the actual dance. Right before the dance, a group of us met up at a friend's house where we took pictures together. There, parents brought out snacks, and we had a bit of a pre-party.

Every single mom—*every single one*—came over to
see if I was okay. Multiple asked if I was eating enough
food. Several asked if I had anorexia. They flat out asked
me. I hadn't even let myself think those words so for them
to look at me and ask that in front of my peers humiliated
me. I acted out of anger and gave snippy responses. I
didn't know what else to say. This was not the night for
conversations like these. I needed a way out. Every angled
look toward me expressed concern, sometimes even anger.
Some let me go. Others didn't. I'm aware of three people
who called my mom that very evening, though I'm sure
more reached out in concern.

Prom only consists of memories in which I am
watched over and observed. I don't remember anything
else. While my peers jetted off to after parties, sipping on
hidden beers and relaxing in sweatpants with formal
clothes tossed about, I requested my date take me home.
He, being a kind human being, took time away from his
evening to drive the thirty minutes, ensuring I got home
safe. This is one of the first moments of countless times in
which I took advantage of others, knowing they were too
scared to turn me down in fear of making my downward
spiral even worse.

The summer of 2013, I lived my life inside my head.
Everything revolved around exercise and keeping a strict
food regimen. It was the time of my first job, giving me the
ability to avoid family meals, eating only when I was off
work. My job as a movie theatre employee required little to
no brain work. I pressed buttons, smiled, made easy
conversation, and coasted through the day. Consequently, I
devoted my mental energy toward considering my body
and how to lose more weight without even anyone else
knowing.

An unexpected advantage of the job was that my
coworkers were all new to my life, resulting in no one

actually knowing me or my journey. They all assumed I'd always looked like this. No one needed to know about the previously lost forty pounds, nor did they need to understand I was on track to lose several more. They either assumed the body I had was the body I was meant to have or they were like me and gave the job absolute zero mindfulness. A lot of coworkers favored working with me actually because I always opted to clean the movie theatres, one of the three areas we all rotated through. Cleaning the specific theatres themselves rather than stationed at the box office or the concession stands meant constantly moving around—walking up and down the stairs, sweeping, a bit of heavy lifting. It required physical exertion, whereas the other two stations primarily resulted in mental exhaustion only.

At work, I found peace. No one sat me down with concerned comments of worry. I clocked in, clocked out, occasionally had friendly conversations with coworkers, and minded my own business.

On a groggy summer afternoon, I came in for a shift apart from the usual shifts my coworkers were used to. Being the only minor on the team, I was not allowed to stay past midnight. A coworker of mine asked why I came in at the odd hour, and I explained it was because of my age. He, along with the two others present at the concession stand, looked at me in shock.

"You're a minor?"

"Yes, I'm sixteen," I said, not even looking up at them. I stood, bent over a drawer, refilling the popcorn bags. "I turn seventeen in a few weeks."

"No way," one of them replied.

I finished the task, met his gaze, and shrugged my shoulders. "Can't change the year I was born."

This incited a conversation and subsequent game we played throughout the shift. It was a slower day, allowing us to take the time to chat with guests at the theatre. Every so often, when a friendly pair came up to buy a snack or two, one of my coworkers took advantage of the situation, pointed to me, and asked the people at hand, "How old do you think Julia is?"

Taking the inquiry too seriously, every one of them looked me up and down as I stood with an awkward grin on me, hands pressed together, awaiting the age in response.

"Twenty-seven."

"Thirty-two?"

"Thirty-five."

Only one person was even remotely close. Her response was "twenty-three." At the time, I took this as an ego boost, assuming my weight loss made me seem mature and womanly. Only now do I look back at this scene in my memory and realize it was only because I had no fat on my face. I look withered and decayed, almost wrinkled.

Working at the movie theatre also gave me the advantage of constantly lying to my parents. Both my schedule and my paycheck went directly to my own accounts. If I said I worked one day, no one was the wiser. I'd often tell them I was going to watch a movie, when really I drove to a nearby park to run an additional few miles, on top of the compulsory five I did every morning at five in the morning. I couldn't stop. It energized me. It thrilled me.

My brain rewired, thriving off the nourishment of my sweat rather than food. The more I exercised, the better I felt. The less I ate, the better I felt.

At this point, I ate a disgustingly low amount. What I lacked in calories ingested, I made up for with copious baking. When not at work, I scoured Pinterest for hours on end, salivating at the food photography, calculating the calories of decadent recipes, giving myself the slight hope

I'd actually bake something for myself, all the while knowing I never would.

I soured those experiences of my childhood, knowing my mom sat in the other room aware of my bad habits, hoping for a change. I would bake dozens of treats, passing them off to coworkers, unsuspecting of any indirect reasoning I had. They thought I was generous. Really, it was an easy excuse to be so near to the food. I grew obsessed with smelling food. I convinced myself that smelling food was nearly the same as tasting it.

The act of denying my hunger, coupled with the incessant preoccupation I felt for food was the dilemma and crowning achievement of my life for my time with anorexia.

To a disordered mind, that may work. Regardless of what my mind craved though, my body didn't catch up to speed. My body still required calories and nourishment, but I no longer felt the desire to acquiesce. Losing more weight had nothing to do with willpower. If anything, the time when I was at the worst with my eating disorder was when I had the least amount of willpower. Make no mistake, having an eating disorder has nothing to do with inner strength or a strong sense of control, it's about feeling like you're drowning and you'll grasp at anything for a sense of stability. It's only when you're out of it you're able to see.

I wanted to talk about it all the time, but I never wanted to say anything. It became my intensely, secretive obsession. People continued to praise me, and I soaked it all in, but indulged in a humble tone of gratitude. I fooled everyone. I don't think I intentionally was this self-absorbed, but it is the only way I can think back on it right now. Positive comments fueled me, acting as a replacement for any nourishment I deprived myself of. Validation was my subsistence.

Any meal I chose to eat was always somehow inadequate.

Eating disorders, as I've mentioned, and I'm hoping the reader well knows by now, have nothing to do with the aesthetic beauty of the body. That's why no one stops at his or her goal weight. Eating disorders are commonly a manifestation of underlying problems. I certainly thought the problem was my body, but it had much more to do with my constant seeking of perfectionism. My lifetime of seeking out validation, coupled with my sexual trauma, lead to the onset of my anorexia. Not my goal weight. I wanted to be perfect, to disappear, to have the physical manifestation of silence. Somehow, this translated to not eating.

Midway through this summer, it was time for my annual doctor's appointment. Already hesitant for the conversations meant to ensure, I avoided any mention of it. I hoped somehow my mom would forget what day it was and we could pass by the appointment entirely. Obviously, that didn't work. My physician had me step on the scale to which I saw a number that no sixteen-year-old should ever weigh.

Preparing myself for a condemnatory conversation about my weight, I started the conversation myself.

"I think it's just because I started running more this summer."

"Oh, you run?" she replied, glancing up from the clipboard.

"Yup. I worked my way up to five miles."

"That's impressive," she nodded, writing a note down.

I looked at my mom. There was that nod of approval again. I hadn't expected that response.

"You are at a lower weight than we'd like to see," she continued, "but I'm not too concerned about it."

My shoulders relaxed. I hadn't even realized they tensed up.

"Does she need to do anything?" My mom asked from the corner of the room.

"Do you feel good?" The doctor asked me.

"I feel great," I responded with a smile. This was true. I did feel good. I felt great, actually.

"Are you menstruating?"

A stream of panic hit my fingertips. This was the question that would find me out.

"I am not. Or, at least, I haven't gotten one in a while."

"How long is a while?" She asked, not looking too distressed though.

"Few months maybe?" This was a lie. Over a year passed since I'd had my last period.

"Hmm," she began, pulling out a BMI chart laminated and pressed in the folds of other generic medical charts. She handed it to me, and I gave it a thorough onceover, trying to convince her I didn't already have the entire image memorized. I knew exactly where I was at on the BMI scale, and I knew exactly where she'd want me to be.

"Let's have you try to put on a few pounds and see if that brings your period back. Put a few scoops of avocado on your sandwiches. Drink an extra glass of chocolate milk after you run. You're young and active, so I'm not too concerned about it."

With that, I was free to leave. We set up a return appointment a month later for me to come in and have her check my progress, but she wasn't too concerned. Neither seemed my mom. In fact, both she and I seemed the same amount of relieved.

I raised my daily intake by a hundred calories. I honestly cannot say whether I was foolish enough to believe this worked or if I was too succumbed in the disorder to do anything else. I choose to believe the latter option, but honestly, it could be either.

As the fateful day of my return appointment grew closer and closer, I started to have arguments with my mom. She lashed out at me, telling me that I was not giving the process any real effort. I confidently told her I was and that she just hadn't seen me do so. All the while, inside my head I was bursting at the seams, knowing I was only going to get in more trouble. I looked in the mirror and could see I was only making negative progress. I was getting thinner and thinner by the day.

A month passed and the morning of the appointment busted into my life. I couldn't avoid it. I walked out into the kitchen where my mom prepared eggs. Without saying a word, I burst out into tears.

"Don't worry," she said, scrambling the yellow mixture together. "I put garlic salt and regular salt in this. It will help you retain water."

Usually, I ate oatmeal or fruit for breakfast. When I looked down at the skillet and understood that the meal was meant for me, I was furious. Upon hearing the motive behind the eggs and seeing my mom was actually trying to get me out of trouble, I relaxed. I continued to cry, but I ate it through the tears.

We drove to the doctor's office soon after, getting there almost a half hour early. My mom shut off the ignition and we sat in silence. As the only car in the parking lot, I had nothing to look at. I rolled up the sleeves of my sweatshirt. It was ninety degrees out, but I did everything to weigh even an ounce more.

"Here," my mom said as she passed me a water bottle.

It took me a second, but I quickly caught on. Drinking water would add to my weight. There was a reason I always weighed myself first thing after using the restroom in the morning. I powered through the water bottle in seconds. Silently, my mom handed me another.

Three water bottles down, enough time had passed for us to step inside to the doctor's office. More cars arrived in the lot, and people bustled around us. My mom opened her car door, but I paused to take a minute to breathe through the pain. The bloat I experienced made me feel as though I would vomit it all out. I thanked my earlier self for wearing multiple layers as I felt my distended stomach underneath the fleece.

After checking in, we went straight to the scale, knowing this was the sole reason for being there. I weighed one pound more than what I weighed the month before. Based on that, I was not sure what sort of response I'd receive from either the doctor or my mom. My mom would reserve her uncensored thoughts until we were out of the doctor's office.

"Great job," my doctor said, jotting down the new number. "Obviously, I'd like to see you gain a few more pounds, but one pound in a month is a healthy rate. Keep it up."

With that, I was handed a pamphlet on healthy fats and sent on my way.

I got into the car with my mom, and she said nothing. I don't know whether she was upset or content. Either way, neither of us were in trouble, so we were better off avoiding any further conversation.

Blurred memories and losing control.

FROM SEPTEMBER TO NOVEMBER OF 2013, when I was seventeen years old and a senior in high school, I abhorred the idea of recovery. My parents fed me what they believed was an adequate amount of food, and I protested, threw tantrums, secretly hid food, and exercised behind their backs. I wasn't having any part of recovery. No aspect of recovery enticed me. My mind, imprisoned as it was, couldn't fathom a better life existing for myself.

On the first day of my senior year, I came home to a furious mother. She snipped at me, asking how my day was. I trod lightly, not knowing what was to come next. Apparently, by the time my first-period class ended, the administrative office called, expressing the school's concern. My mom was furious with me. I attempted to protest, claiming the school was overreacting. Little did she know that I'd spent the day reiterating that same lie to all of my teachers and several peers. I even tried out the lie of, *"I had some medical issues this summer; that's why I look like this,"* just to see how the sounds rolled off my tongue. Turns out, it could have been a handy lie, had I started it sooner. I let myself go for too long for it to actually linger as a fraction of the truth for anyone else.

"Don't play games with me, Julia."

"It's not a big deal," I said, edging my way out of the living room.

"How could you let it get this bad?" she stammered, half-yelling, half-begging tears to retreat.

I, unable to hold back my own tears, stammered back in protest, "I don't know. I'm sorry. I don't know what you want me to do."

"Look at you," she said, throwing her hands up. I assumed she did so in disgust. "You're nothing."

She wasn't wrong. On top of my school's polo, I wore a child's size medium sweater. I wrapped a ponytail around the waistband of my uniform skirt, just so it would stay on. I withered away to nothing, but couldn't confront that truth. Hidden away in a folder I dare not look at in an old laptop of mine is a picture of me on this day. I shudder every time I look at it.

"You need to gain weight. Now."

"I'm trying." I offered, knowing that would only upset her further. It did.

"No, you're not." She yelled. "Look at the pain you're causing everyone around you."

At that, I walked away, too ashamed of the blunt truth of that statement. I was causing everyone pain. Everyone, I believed, would have it so much easier if I wasn't there destroying the peace. Everyone around me ate easily and normally; for me to not do so was ridiculous. I knew that well enough, but that couldn't change the glitches in my brain.

This was my senior year, and I knew that any shot at freedom had slipped away before I even had the chance to settle into the new year.

My mom screamed after me, but I couldn't face her. Instead, I stormed into the kitchen, grabbed three protein bars, poured myself a glass of milk, and sat outside on the steps on our back porch. I chomped my way through the food, swallowing just as many tears as food. A primitive urge in me came out, devouring the food as though my life depended on it, and it very well might have, at that point. I hadn't eaten anything that day. I gulped the milk in two full swoops, nauseating myself.

Soon after, she came out. I flung the empty wrappers at her, showed her the melted chocolate stains on my fingers, proclaiming, "See? See?"

She looked at me in disgust, full fury. "How do I know you didn't just chuck the food somewhere out here?"

I broke down, more hysterical than ever.

"Why can't you just believe me?" I pleaded.

"You're killing yourself. I don't know what I'm supposed to do. You told me you had it under control this summer and it is only getting worse."

With that, she took off back into the house, leaving me crouched down on the floor as I mangled all the foiled wrappers. Every inch of me begged myself to throw up all the food, not out of disordered chaos but from the rapid rate at which I ate the food.

I sat outside for hours. My dad came home, saw me playing with the grass, and gave me a look.

"How was the first day of senior year?" He asked me as though the blotchy blush on my cheeks were as normal as the freckled-specks.

"Ask mom," I replied in my teenage angst.

Minutes later, my mom came outside. "Dinner's ready. Get inside."

Usually, I watched her prepare dinner like a surgeon observing a student—careful to ensure no slips of the hand occurred. My mom always refused to use measuring cups, but by this point in my disorder, I was able to gauge pours and scoops with impeccable accuracy. Based on my observations, I was able to tally up a caloric amount as well as determine what my portion size should be. I had a hand in everything, even if I wasn't physically touching the food.

On this night, dinner happened without my consent, without my knowledge, without my careful, meticulous consolations. I walked in to see pasta draining in the sink. Ravioli. Okay, I thought to myself; ravioli, I can do. I knew the exact amount of ravioli I always had. This was an easy meal to calculate and feel safe in. My gaze transferred over to the sauce simmering on the stove. Meat sauce. There was no separate pot for traditional marinara sauce, as I typically had with this meal. I couldn't deal with the meat and the oil and fatty grease I could taste with each bite on the ravioli.

"Where is my sauce?" The question came out of me before I could hold it in. I knew I was in for it already, so I knew it best not to make it worse. I couldn't help it, though. At that point, it was not me talking—it was my eating disorder.

"You'll have your dinner just like the rest of us," said my mom as she grabbed plates.

I looked to my dad, but he quickly looked away, refusing eye contact with me just as well.

"Okay," I whispered, not to them, but to myself. One dinner, I remember thinking to myself. I can do one dinner. I walked over to grab my plate and scoop out my pre-planned portion, but my mom swooped in between myself and the food.

"Sit down."

"Why?"

"I'm going to bring you your plate."

I tried to look at my dad again, but I knew there was no way getting around this. One meal, I reminded myself. I can make it through one meal. The protein bars rested in my stomach, hunkering me down as though each bar was a slab of poundage adding itself on, minute by minute.

The white porcelain bowl brought to me by my mom was double my normal portion. Combined with the addition of the meat sauce as opposed to standard marinara, I didn't know how I'd get through the meal. The real kicker, though, was the glass of milk my mom brought out after.

"Please don't." I tried.

"No. You don't get to do that."

"But, I already had milk today."

"And you should have another glass. You should have more food than I gave you, too. Don't push it, young lady."

With that, she placed the milk in front of me, sat down with her own meal, and waited. My dad waited too. My brother, oblivious to it all or just playing ignorant, dug in to his own meal. I prodded the ravioli with my fork, as though checking to ensure its lack of life. I took a bite, hoping actually eating might mitigate the fears— sometimes, that worked. However, I was only further horrified when I bit into meat ravioli. We always had cheese ravioli. This was not a part of the meal my mom anticipated or did so to spite my disorder even more. She simply bought the wrong ravioli. I didn't know this at the time though. I assumed this was a malicious choice.

"It's meat ravioli."

"Deal with it."

"No, I can't eat this."

"You will."

"No, I don't like it."

"Honestly, Julia, I don't really care."

Following that, I tried to eat it. I took a few more items, and methodically chewed and chewed, hoping to aid the digestion process as much as possible, assuming this would help me get rid of it all. I don't know where that thread of ill-thought-out logic came about, but in those moments of eating what I feared, I latched onto anything that made me even an ounce more comfortable.

Halfway through the silent meal, I looked to my mom and dad.

"Can I be done?"

I'd managed about half the ravioli, nearly none of the meat sauce, and not a drop of the milk.

"Are you serious?"

"Yes," I said so quickly, "please."

"No you need to finish," My dad chimed in.

"Drink your milk," my mom added.

"I can't do this. I really can't."

"You are no longer in charge of what you can and can't do, Julia." My mom said, "We will decide your meals. We will decide what you eat. We will decide how much you eat. We will decide when you are done with a meal. You are not done with this meal."

In came the tears again. "We don't have to do that. I can fix this. I can make myself better."

"No," my dad said, slamming his fist down on the table. "We let you try all summer, and nothing changed. You only got worse. So unless you want to stay at a hospital, you need to sit here and finish your meal and finish every other meal until you are normal again."

"Please, no," I wept, barely audible to the others at the table.

I received no response, which incited in me a furious response. I needed to be heard. I needed to win this fight. I was not about to relinquish any and all control to people who had no thought for nutrition. They wouldn't take care of me, I told myself. They would let me get fat.

I sat there for another few minutes, not touching my food, picking at a scab on my scalp.

"Eat," my mom said.

Unable to hold in the anxiety and the nausea, I threw my pasta plate across the table, smashing against the wall. Sauce flung everywhere. My brother stood up and said, "Okay, I am done."

I started crying even more, which I didn't think was possible at that point, but the body goes to extreme ends while in crisis.

"I'm so sorry," I managed to get out.

"The time for 'sorry' has passed," my dad said. "You have to eat."

With that, they portioned out another bowl of pasta, similar in size to the first bowl. I had already eaten half of the first bowl. I thought it was insane for them to act as if I'd eaten nothing. Not another word came out of my mouth, though. I sat there and ate every speck, fearing the additional food that would come if I acted out again.

I hovered over to the sink in a daze. The terrifying realization came to mind that I'd eaten more in the past four hours than I had in the past four days. Just that thought alone made me want to purge everything, down to the bible I knew would come up if I pushed myself too far. I didn't, though, not out of strength, but out of the knowledge that my parents would drive me straight to a hospital if I did anything callous again that evening.

Though not even 8:00 pm, I went straight to bed. I sat there, contemplating exercise, but with a bloated stomach in tow, I knew it would only make me sicker, more aware of the physical discomfort in my body. Instead, I opted to go straight to bed and wake up early to exercise.

The morning came sooner than I ever wanted, but I bolstered myself with the excitement of a run. A chance to burn calories. I needed it desperately so. I threw on a sports bra, a sweatshirt, and some socks. I tiptoed out to the kitchen when I was greeted by kitchen lights already on, and my mom standing in the kitchen.

"No running. You're done with that. What do you want for breakfast? You can have waffles with syrup, or toast with jam."

"But—" I tried, but she gave me not an inch.

"Waffles or toast?" she repeated. "Or, we can talk about hospitals."

Going to a hospital was the absolute last option for me, for a variety of reasons. The main reason for this was simply because I didn't want people knowing. If I went to a hospital, I'd have to take time out school, which meant not going to college on time. I needed college. College was the one thing keeping me going. College meant a fresh start. It meant not being surrounded by all of this hurt, by all of the trauma and toxicity.

Also, going to the hospital for treatment meant I was truly out of control. If I stayed at home, I still had some leeway. I had my car. I had my job. I had the comfort of already knowing the meals my mom made. Yes, she'd be in charge of the quantity, but I knew the ingredients by heart and could make pretty quick estimations. Knowing how many calories I was eating would always provide a semblance of peace, even if it was far more than I could happily ingest.

Finally, going to a treatment center at a hospital meant others could know. You see, all this time, I'd convinced myself that no one outside of me knew I had a problem. I had truly blinded myself to the looks other people gave me, the whispers of concern. Most people went on talking to me like nothing had changed, and even though I was well aware of the gossip behind my back, ignorance was bliss. If no one said anything, and if I didn't do anything about it, I could go along my merry way eating practically nothing and exercising myself to death. If I left for treatment, I would torture myself with the constant wondering of what others thought of me. Of course, that ship had sailed. I was emaciated beyond belief, and I knew everyone immediately associated my name with "anorexic," already, but because I'd been able to continue on as though everything was normal, I'd convinced myself all was well.

The decision of what to have for breakfast was seemingly impossible, but the thought of actually doing something about my disorder was that much more daunting. So, I did a quick calculation. My mom probably meant two slices of toast. I looked at the bread she had in front of her. Whole wheat. That particular brand was 100 calories per slice. The jelly we had in the fridge was 50 calories per tablespoon. The waffles on hand were 190 calories for two waffles. The syrup was 200 calories per ¼ cup.

"Who gets to pour the syrup?" I asked.

"You can," she replied. "I will watch, though."

"Who gets to spread the jelly?"

"I do."

I considered this for a second. My mom folded her arms, clearly already impatient with me.

"Toast," I replied. This was the safer option, I'd concluded. Even though I was in control of how much syrup I poured, I didn't want to find myself in a situation where she said I hadn't poured enough, and then wind up pouring even more than I'd tally in that initial estimate. But, if my mom spread the jelly on the toast before I ate it, I'd have a much better chance at accurately counting it all up. Knowing the calories was always the safer option for me. Even if the option was less calories by far, I always opted for the option that I knew for certain how many calories I was eating.

The toast she made had just a little over a tablespoon of jelly on each slice, rounding out my breakfast to about 350 calories. Surprised by this, I ate it relatively unphased. Then, she brought out a Starbucks bottled drink. 180 calories. I gave a pleading look to my mom, to which she responded by opening up the bottle and handing it to me.

"You drink this," she said, "and then you go to school."

School. Ah, yes school. I could at least have a few hours away, uncontrolled by the food requirements of my mom. I was only two meals in and already exhausted. I drank the iced coffee, hating myself for finding the meal tasty. Glancing at the clock, I was shocked to find over an hour passed. I jogged to the back of the house, threw on articles of clothing that passed the uniforms requirements, and made a beeline for the door. I didn't say goodbye, but my mom stopped me, shoving a bag of peanuts in my hands.

"You are to eat this before you come home for lunch. Do you hear me?"

"Yes," I replied, walking out.

As I drove to school, I waited until I was far enough away from my house before rolling down the window and tossing the bag of peanuts out the side. This became a morning ritual for months.

Being that it was my senior year, I only had five classes, giving me the opportunity to go home right before the lunch bell. The previous year, I'd looked forward to this, already dreaming of it as the perfect excuse to tell my friends, "Oh, I eat at home," and to tell my parents, "Oh, I ate at school," and using that time in between to go for an additional run. Based on the earlier comment for my mom, however, I knew that wouldn't fly.

I came home that day to a turkey sandwich, slathered with mayo and paired with two slices of cheese. On white bread. This last aspect was the demise of my entire body. I'd demonized white bread to the fullest, equating it to an incarnation of Satan, essentially.

The more I talked to my mom, the worse it got. Instead of even trying to start something, I sat down to eat it. It tasted quite nice. My mom put on the TV, already unenthused with the job she assigned herself of watching me. She put on "Say Yes to the Dress," a show that brings nostalgic, loving memories for both of us. It seemed as though it was a peace treaty of some kind. Rather than taking the bait, though, I took advantage of it. While she watched the show, I started to rip bits and pieces of the sandwich off, shoving them into my socks.

In utter glee, I surprised myself with how much I was able to get into my socks. The milk my mom paired with my sandwich was unavoidable, so I drank that fine enough, smiling to myself about the second loophole I already found.

Over the next several weeks, I continued to find loopholes. My parents started to purchase whole milk for me. My brother always drank 1% milk. When they weren't looking though, I, without fail, switched the milks. My brother, none the wiser, was the perfect partner in crime for this. To counteract the increase in calories I was eating, I started to wake up 3 am in the morning to exercise in my room. I repeated the same videos over and over. I started to do plank holds while watching videos on Instagram a-la-Buzzfeed-Tasty, where people made decadent desserts. It was my new obsession, replacing the wasteful hours I browsed Pinterest. This was more interactive and felt more real. Plus, it was easy to perch my phone up while in a plank hold and zone out to the brownie batter pouring over a pan.

At 6 o'clock on the dot, my mom stood in her bathroom waiting to weigh me. This was where another loophole came into the mix. With my mind on the summer's doctor appointment, I thought back to when my mom gave me the water bottles to drink. Foolproof plan. I then exercised from 3:00 am-5:30 am, and spent the following half hour in the bathroom, guzzling bottles of water. At my worst, I got up to seven water bottles of water. Each and every time though, I started to get really blurry vision. My stomach distended so far out that I had to wear a sweatshirt for it to unnoticed. I then took advantage of the baggy sweatshirt, filling my bra with bottles of nail polish and anything else small enough and yet dense enough to make a dent in my weight.

Because of all of this, my parents were under the impression that I was gaining weight. In reality, I was losing even more weight. At the time, I didn't know what was happening to me, but I was likely suffering from refeeding syndrome. This is when someone who is undernourished all of a sudden is exposed to more nutrients, but the body does not know how to react. For me, this resulted in terrible night sweats. I woke up drenched in sweat, to the point where I often confused it for wetting myself. Additionally, the refeeding syndrome made me lose more weight. I didn't know this, though, because my only way of knowing how much I weighed was the faulty weigh-in I did with my mom every day.

In those months, exhaustion overtook me. This wasn't the sort of physical exhaustion one would expect from abusing my body as I had, but rather emotional and psychological exhaustion. I couldn't walk through a room, whether at home, at school, or at work, where I didn't feel every pair of eyes scan over my physique. This was how I knew I was only getting worse. Even though I ate more, my progress was nonexistent.

At school, no one bothered to hide their whispers after a while. What initially attracted me to indulge in my eating disorder was the ease of isolation and setting myself apart. I was tapped into this part of the world that was all my own, one I could escape into and soak up my own special time away from the harsh realities I refused to confront. It was only until I fell below society's ideal body weight where people disrupted this faulty paradise (which, is a *whole other* issue that I hope to address. My eating disorder needed attention and intervention an entire year before this, when my BMI was not of concern).

During this time, I stopped talking entirely. As a result of my self-imposed, rather dramatic muteness, alongside the increased nutrition, my mind became hypervigilant on observing everything around me. I lived in the same house for twelve years, but in this short period of time, I felt like I looked around for the first time. Also, I spent more time with my cat.

The following anecdote I'm about to share sounds silly. I get it. But, for my mind at the time, incredibly stunted as it was, needed to make this connection. This is the first time I can look back at my recovery and realized I made a step, though minuscule as it was, toward a better future for myself. It was the first time in over a year where I could honestly reflect and realize I was being self-aware. This is the story of how my family's cat, Snickers, made me take *my first* step toward recovery.

Even though she is an indoor cat, our little feline contracted fleas, somehow. They were everywhere. Our once hyperactive kitty was now lethargic, resorting to multiple naps throughout the day. We eventually had to get our house fumigated, which was a nightmare in itself. After our house was finally flea-free, we thought we could move on from this. Not true.

Snickers, by that point, habitually bit and scratched herself to the point of piercing through her skin in various areas. Portions of her fur were licked clean, revealing her skin. My family grew concerned for Snick, and my dad drove her to the vet. There, she received her lovely cone of shame. She was furious. Snickers began to hiss and whack at us every time we would try to extend some love toward her. She could not understand that we just wanted her to get better.

She was a fighter, but eventually, she just gave up, resorting to sleeping through every day.

Eventually the wounds healed, and my dad felt it was time to give her the freedom that she deserved. As soon as he took off the cone though, she began to gnaw at the point on her body that had previously been scathed. We all looked at each other in confusion. She was healed (or so we thought) so why was she still hurting herself?

My dad decided that she was not ready to have the cone off, and it was immediately put back on. Needless to say, our little kitty was pissed. She wanted the freedom, but she could not handle it.

She hated the cone, but she could not refrain from hurting herself when the cone was away.

She was only supposed to have the cone for three weeks, and she has had it for almost three months now.

One day I looked at her and thought to myself, "We are going through the exact same thing."

My cone of shame is my eating disorder. It is the thing I loathe most in my life, and without it, I could live a beautiful, positive life. I know this. I know I could go on and live a wonderful life once I release my eating disorder, but for some reason, whenever my "cone" gets taken off, I freak out. Watching my parents constantly frustrated with my cat gives me insight into how they view my disorder. They do not want to get angry with her for biting herself. They just want her to stop. They do not want to get angry with me for not eating properly. They just want me to get better.

It may seem like a strange comparison with no real linkage, but for me, it gave me an inkling of courage to fight. Her stubborn fight shed light on truth existing outside of myself. Perhaps, I realized, there were parts of the world's veracity I was unable to see for myself. Perhaps, I considered, recovery would help me see those aspects. I continued to watch my family watch the cat. I saw how frustrated they were with her. I saw how frustrated they were with me. Snicker was ignorant of the damage she caused herself. Odd as it was, the flea-stricken cat was the first thing I found myself able to relate to. Her cone of shame became a defining step in my recovery.

During those months, I gained *maybe* three pounds. That was only after my body had adjusted to refeeding syndrome. In total, I'd lost probably an additional ten pounds. I was on a quick route to killing myself and more miserable than ever because I had no control. The hiding food in my socks aspect wasn't thrilling me. It'd become too easy. The water loading was just miserable physically, and it no longer was a trick, but something I had to maintain if I didn't want my parents to freak out.

It wasn't until I looked at Snickers and made this connection I realized how insufficient my progress was. Prior, I thought I had summited Mt. Kilimanjaro. I remember feeling aghast at how no one was praising me for all the progress I made. (Eating disorders made me a self-centered, high and mighty bitch. There is no getting around that. I was awful.)

Gaining three pounds in three months was not recovery. If anything, that was water weight or natural weight fluctuation. I knew I was kidding myself and fooling everyone around me. It wasn't until I look at that silly cat I realized my apathetic attempt at recovery was unacceptable.

That very same day, I upped my caloric intake. I didn't hide any food in my socks. I did not stop that behavior in a day, but I made the consecrated effort to reduce it. Over the span of a month, I stopped completely. I learned to take off my cone of shame. I entertained the idea of finally giving myself a break from the disease and allowing myself to enjoy life.

The question I receive by and large the most is, "how did you do it?" "How did you recover?" This question frustrates me—not because it's asked, but because my answer comes across blunt and emotionless. It has to do with removing any sense of faith and hope from my life and choosing to redefine my necessary actions in this life.

For me to "do it," I needed to take a stark break from my eating disorder. My anorexia utterly consumed my mind with each passing thought. Find something else to contemplate, to look forward to. It nourishes the mind to relax and dream of a brighter future. I do not know how to tell anyone "how to recover." There is no one set way other than to just eat and break every disordered rule set in the brain. Once I began to nourish myself with actual food, give my body a physical rest, and settle into a decent caloric intake, the mental cloud faded away. I was able to participate in conversations and interact with what was going on around me. It felt incredible.

So how did I do it? How do I do it now? All I can say is I got tired. I was tired of hoping and having faith that I'd suddenly magically recover. I got tired of my mom crying. I got tired of my dad shouting. I got tired of everyone at school whispering. I got tired of hiding away from the world. The only solution was to eat.

If I did not gain the weight to settle into a healthy range, I would not go to college. The year before I entered into college, when I was at my worst, my parents threatened to make me turn down all college acceptances if I did not pull myself together. I woke up every morning to my mother monitoring my breakfast. I sat at the dining room table, hiding behind my computer reading blog posts from others in the eating disorder community, while I took the tiniest bites of my muffin, utilizing a fork.

One day I looked down at the plate with crumbs everywhere, purposefully done so I could eat less, and I remember thinking to myself, "what am I doing?" Muffins are not meant to be eaten with a fork. I wasn't quite ready to change, but I knew this was not a life worth living.

That day, it took me forty-five minutes to eat a 200 calorie muffin, all the while my mother was lying on the couch glaring at me as my mouth opened and closed timidly. After, I continued on into my disordered routine. Once I had finishing brush my teeth, I walked into my room to see my mother sitting in an upright position, perched on the corner of my bed. My personal zone invaded by what felt like an army of fifty, my guard went up immediately.

"We need to have a talk about your eating habits."

Oh God, I thought to myself, *here we go again.* Every conversation, at the time, was about me, my eating, and how screwed up it all was. I couldn't escape the conversations. I failed her time and time again, but that week, I had eaten all she required of me. I hadn't thrown any pasta bowls or spilled any of my milk. I was complying. Why couldn't she leave me alone?

She told me it was not normal to eat a muffin like that. I didn't understand her concern, and I was not in the mood to deal with this. I started crying, which made her angrier with each tear. She loathed when I would cry; she knew it was a manipulative tactic of mine to attempt to seize the conversation. This time, she was not having it.

"Stop crying and use your words." I felt like I was a three-year-old, but that is how I was acting. I cried even harder.

"Stop crying!" She yelled at me. "Use your words."

As I managed to control my toddler tantrum, I heaved, sighed, and hiccupped, until I finally got out the words, "I hate myself."

I will never forget the look on my mother's face. She looked so heartbroken. Looking back, I cannot imagine how I'd feel if I had a daughter and she told me that she hated herself. What was it like being in her shoes? I destroyed my family during this time. I regret so many of the things I said to her and my father. I regret so many of my actions. Not a day goes by when I don't consider this.

Somehow, she stopped herself from bursting with emotion. She calmed herself, continuing to talk to me. She explained how most normal teenagers would enjoy having to gain weight. "If your brother was told he needed to put on weight, he'd happily be driving through In N Out every day."

I saw in her this deep need for me to adopt that mentality, but all I could muster was, "That is gluttonous."

Fed up, I looked at her with a look that essentially expressed, "I don't know what to tell you anymore." I'd tried to explain. Over and over. All I did was think of ways to adequately convey what it felt like to live in my head, but I couldn't. It's an irrational question, asking someone what anorexia is or why they can't eat. But I felt like I kept getting asked different iterations of that same question repeatedly. I was sick and tired of it. I was sick and tired of myself. I was sick and tired of everything.

Resigned, she looked to me and said, "If you don't clean up your act, there is no way in hell we could send you to college in good conscience." They had said this to me before, but that day, I realized it was true. They meant it. They would keep me there, tied to that bedframe of mine, preoccupied with too many feelings to think straight. Anger instilled in me. If I didn't go to college, what was the point of anything? I poured every ounce of time into studying, learning, performing, making myself a well-rounded individual in order to have a better future. I know many people dream about their wedding days and starting families, but from a very young age, the constant dream I had was my first day of class at university. All I have ever wanted for myself was to read and learn and understand the world around me. There I was only months away from my dream becoming a reality and *I* was throwing it away because my mind took me captive. To have it all taken away from myself because I could not eat like a normal person? It seemed so insipid.

So, I woke up. Not a lot, but at least enough to make a change. I knew I had to give it a shot. I had to put on weight. I had to get to college. I needed a fresh start.

When people ask, "How did you do it?" Here is the truth: I was not strong. Those urges were there constantly. Those urges still are there. My head still screams at me occasionally for the food I eat.

But I *have* to do it. I so wish there were magical words I could recite here with a step-by-step manual on everything one can do to have the perfect recovery, but that doesn't exist. I wish I could cause a light bulb in each and every one of the minds of people who struggle with eating disorders that ignites a fiery passion for recovery, but that will never happen.

I cannot choose recovery for anyone. Everyone around me desperately wanted recovery for me, but I didn't make any genuine progress until I made the decision to try.

I was the only person that allowed myself to get better. I needed other people around me to continually encourage and love on me, but that decision to actually change had to be made by me.

You are the only person that can allow yourself to get better. You are the only thing stopping you from living a better life (if you have the privilege to afford food and the time to focus on your mental health—again, I say this while wholeheartedly recognizing the privileges I have in my life and in my recovery). Every single person around you—family, friends, peers—they crave for you to want to get better. You can go to therapy or inpatient treatment centers or your family can shove food down your throat, but until you establish that positive mentality into your brain, you will never truly recover.

I realized that I was the only thing stopping myself. I had to decide to want to live again.

A cautionary guiding light.

AT THIS POINT, I DON'T KNOW WHAT MADE ME turn to Instagram. Having already had a Tumblr account dedicated to losing weight, I assumed a similar community was to be found on Instagram as well. Instagram, though, had a more user-friendly approaching to surfing tags and exploring different communities. That is how I quickly found the #ed recovery community, alongside all of the companioned hashtags with it. During the times in which I secretly exercise from 3 am in the morning to when the rest of my family woke up, I'd hold a plank for a half hour, while I scrolled through and observed these women around the world enduring the exact same feelings and thoughts, but they were all in different stages of their recovery. Some were like me, faking it and begrudgingly eating only what their parents required of them. Some were actively indulging their eating disorder, eating minimal meals and throwing away food at every opportunity. I sought resonance and comfort there, and I immediately jumped into creating an account.

When I opened my account, I labeled it LordStillLovesMe, because at the time, part of my facade was a wholesome Christian identity. It would take years for me to realize I was using this religious ideal as a crutch for people to like me. I never knew the gravity of what being a practicing Christian mean, and I took it too lightly. It was disrespectful of me, though I had no ill-intent, but, nonetheless, I still did so. I was a Christian because it was cute, acceptable, and popular. Not because I craved Jesus Christ. I just thought it was the right thing to do.

My first hundred or so posts were never about attaining followers or growing a mass attraction for others to watch my recovery. If anything, initially, my recovery account on Instagram was purely a place where I could vent and purge all of the emotions built up inside of me. I thought I might find someone who would come across me and say, *"yes girl, I see you, I get you."* but I didn't need anything more than that. I also, being out of control with my food and having my parents plan all of my meals, felt as though this was a place where I could immortalize the food. If I took pictures, I could sit and mull over what I'd eaten. It would give me a better chance to estimate the amount of calories.

Fully aware of how incompetent my current recovery plan was (by no fault of parents— they had no idea what do. I cannot blame them), I took it upon myself to do some research. I couldn't keep up with the little hours of sleep as well as the hours and hours of exercise while shoveling food into my socks. I quite literally was running out of socks that weren't stained. I was so painfully cold, the type of cold that shivered me into waves of nausea. Lanugo covered my body. This is a symptom of various eating disorders which is a sort of long, downy fur, layering over the body as a futile attempt to bring warmth to the starved lifeform I convinced myself was a healthy physique.

My google search bar became familiar with, "how to recover from anorexia." I received a lot of different answers: veganism, IIFYM, treatment centers, and a variety of other options. Nothing clicked for me. Or, if it did, like IIFYM, I knew my parents would never be okay with it. I had to find something we could all find appropriate.

That's what lead me to Minnie Maud. I first discovered the website, filled with articles and research, as well as an interactive forum for those currently undergoing this form of recovery, at the tail end of October 2013.

The basic tenets of Minnie Maud when I first discovered it (I believe they have changed) are as follows:

- For my age, height, and gender, I was required to eat a minimum of 3,000 calories. The "minimum," was emphasized. If I found myself hungrier for more food, I had to eat more. I could not tell myself no. No food was off limits. There was no maximum for how many calories I ate.
- Under no circumstances was I allowed to exercise. If I had a particularly physical day, be it for work or school, I needed to adjust my minimum to reflect this. I needed to ensure that every single calorie I took in went directly toward restoring my organs and healing all of the damage I'd done.
- Weighing myself was strictly forbidden.

To follow Minnie Maud meant subscribing to those rules. *Why would anyone do this method of treatment?* I remember thinking to myself. This sounded like a surefire way to balloon and become heavier than I ever had been before. At the time the thought of this would turn me suicidal. I could handle a bit of weight gain, but to be heavier than I ever was? Not happening.

The enticing element of Minnie Maud is that it teaches your body to have a healthy metabolic rate again. It resets the metabolism. Minnie Maud is predicated on the promise that the disordered body, once fully immersed in recovery, will find itself settled at a healthy weight, theoretically able to maintain on 3,000 calories. Now, that hooked me. I never thought I'd be able to maintain on a sustainable amount of calories. I didn't even need 3,000 calories. I just needed something higher than what I was initially comfortable with.

Minnie Maud intrigued me. I wasn't ready for it, but I kept the tab open on my computer for weeks.

Those first few months of quasi-recovery were not cute. They were not Instagram worthy. They were filled with uncomfortable bloating, night sweats, tears. With my abdominal muscles torn apart, eaten away as my body took to do anything to keep me alive, my stomach swelled all throughout my recovery. Thanksgiving, in particular, was a horrendous day. It tore my extended family apart. However, that's just what I needed, unfortunately.

I woke up on Thanksgiving morning with determination. We were going over to see my father's side of the family. They are proudly Armenian, therefore, rather than the traditional American fare of mashed potatoes, stuffing, and turkey, we had luleh kabob, boreg, tarak; all of my favorite foods.

Desperately, I wanted to enjoy the meal. I didn't want to be my obvious illness to act as the focus of the evening. I wanted to see my grandparents and my uncle and enjoy the holiday. I wanted the attention to be on everything but me; of course, that was not the case.

The three of them, my grandmother, grandfather, and uncle hadn't seen me since my birthday in August, where even then I was frail. Through November, I steadily had gained a few pounds back, but I was still remarkably emaciated. I was hard to look at. As soon as we stepped into my grandparent's home, a place that often felt like comfort growing up, I knew any hope I built up throughout the day quickly dissipated. All eyes shot at me. My grandparents, without concealment, spoke in Armenian to one another, a language I do not have the privy of fluency to. My dad shot a comment back at them, and everyone grew quiet. Then, the forced hellos and good-to-see-yous began. I cowered as I had to hug everyone. I sat in the corner, speaking only when spoken to as my place in the world soon settled in. Time passed. We sat down to dinner.

My uncle, always a character and always someone I admired, had ignored me throughout the evening. Without prompting, he looked at me from across the table and asked, "So how much do you weigh now, you little skeleton?"

My dad shouted at him, "Enough," to which my uncle laughed.

He replied, "I had a right to ask. She is my niece."

My dad told him with authority to stop, but he didn't. He kept it going. My grandfather attempted a joke, but it fell on loose ears as he tried switching gears to an altogether different conversation. Everyone at the table either looked at my uncle, my dad, or the ceiling. A great wave of annoyance fell through the air. Before, there had been a slight chance the night could be enjoyed by some. That quick exchanged ruined it all.

I looked down at my plate, instantly disgusted with myself. I saw the quantity of food and felt overwhelmed. It was a decent portion, by no means enough to make me gain weight. Had I eaten it all, I would have been insanely proud of myself. I couldn't eat it anymore though.

The conversation stalled between my uncle and my dad as my grandmother told them both to stop the nonsense and eat their food. I looked to my dad who nodded encouragingly. I looked down at my plate again. I picked up my fork, my body convulsed. Wanting absolutely no more attention, I begged my body to stop shaking. No one spoke. My family all stared down at their own meals, picking at the salad.

Again, I looked to my dad. He mouthed, "Are you okay?"

I nodded a resounding "yes." For once, I didn't want to be the problem child. Not that day. Not again. I'd been the problem for so long that all I wanted was for one damn night to not be about me and my issues. I was trying. I hadn't made progress, but I could feel my mind headed in the right direction. I knew I was en route to wanting to do better. To not have everyone around me wonder and worry.

My dad gave me a grim shake of his head, accepting my quiet lie. I took the first bite of my meal. I zoned out to everything in the world and all that was on the plate, robotic and without thought. The dinner passed by in a blurry haze after that first bite; I don't recall tasting any of it.

To this day, I haven't eaten any of those foods, partly because if I'm being quite honest (and I might as well be, considering that this is a memoir of sorts), these foods trigger me more than any other meal I can imagine. These foods, what once was childhood favorites are now imbued with a time of utter hopelessness. I think about these items, the night, the manifestation of my family's strength decaying, and it takes all of me not to burst into guilt-ridden tears.

In my time of recovery, I've overcome a lot of fears. I've healed in a lot of places and memories. This is not one of them.

What brought me out of my daze was the tune of my grandmother singing, "Dessert time!" as though the past half hour hadn't transpired in uncomfortable silence.

For a third time, I looked over to my dad. He declared, "I think we are going to go home."

This infuriated my grandmother. She went off, half in Armenian and half in English, shouting that he was making a big deal out of nothing. It was stupid to go home and would do more harm than good. My dad didn't respond, only whispering to my brother to grab his jacket. My brother and my mom each didn't say a word, knowing they played no role in this, and just followed orders and headed directly outside to the car.

As I put on my own jacket, I hunched over, minimizing the attention I refused to acknowledge sprayed all over me. My dad stood between his parents and me. We walked to the car as I sobbed.

Outside of the car, back at our own home, my dad cupped my face into his hands, giving me a reaction I wasn't expecting. I was so used to hurting both him and my mom; I thought I was in for a yelling. I deserved that. I knew that. The entire car ride home I prepared myself for it. Before he said a thing I cried out over and over, "I am so sorry. I am so sorry."

His only response, "No."

I cried even more, knowing I'd truly crossed a line that night. But then, he said something that surprised me.

"They were in the wrong. Not you. I am proud of you. They were inconsiderate." He said. I cried even more. He moved his hands from my face to my shoulders, slightly shaking me. "I will never let anyone talk to my daughter like that. Not even them."

He protected me that night. I thought for so long I was fighting the battle alone, but he showed me was truly there. I'm so thankful for him on this night. He always protected me. Always. This is the night I care about it the most, though.

My entire life, my dad was the one I wanted to impress the most. I don't know why, but somewhere along the way I set up that expectation for myself. As a result, we found ourselves always struggling to have the difficult conversations. I often cry around him. I don't know why I do so. I fear I'll never, even now, be able to live up to what he needs in a daughter. Even now, as healed as I am, I fear

I went too far once; I'll never fully return to his good graces. He gave up contact with his family after this night. For me. Because I wasn't strong enough to eat my favorite meal. I started something that day. It still is not mended. Not entirely.

Some parts of recovery are more difficult to grieve and heal from. This is one of them for me.

My dad took me in his arms and hugged me. He then pulled away, forcing me to look him in the eyes again.

"Are you okay?"

His own eyes red, myself sobbing, I shook my head no and apologized again. I was so sorry.

I went to the bathroom to change out of my clothes, but also to gain control of my emotions. I was in hysterics. I looked at myself in the mirror and fully observed the monster I'd let myself become.

In those moments, I realized I wasn't destroying myself. I was destroying my family.

I monopolized their holidays and their times of rest. I'd never seen my parents more anxious in their entire lives. This created an internal switch in me.

I realized the very profound, if morbid concept: I could hate myself all I wanted, but I felt no thrill in hurting my family.

That wasn't fair.

I had no self-worth. That, I would be okay with. But my parents deserved none of it. They didn't ask for it.

At the time, I couldn't see that I also did not deserve it nor did I ask for it, but that ounce of reality made me want to do better, to be better.

I went back out into the kitchen, grabbed three protein bars, poured myself a large cup of whole milk with two scoops of bulking protein power. Pounding away the food without a moment's thought, I felt how easy it was. In thinking of my family, eating became simpler. Not easy as though I didn't struggle at all, but easy enough to hold down the swallows. I grabbed one more protein bar for good measure.

This was the start of fully seeping into Minnie Maud recovery.

Make no mistake, once I started Minnie Maud, it did not mean I could fully give into my cravings. I didn't eat 3,000 calories guilt-free every day. Although, if memory serves me, once I made the switch to committing to Minnie Maud, it did become easier. I set a goal for myself every day and I knew I had to hit it. I was so exhausted of seeing my mom cry, so I just did it. I figured I had no other choice so I might as well see what actually putting work into my recovery looked like.

Before I go any further into my experience with Minnie Maud, I need to clarify one thing: I am not saying Minnie Maud is *the* right way to recover. Advocating for one right way to recover, an ideal of sorts, is a symptom of the illness itself. I found myself falling into this mentality during parts of my recovery, but ultimately, now I can say that doing so—regardless of the method of recovery— shifts perfectionism into a new form. For me, that was one of the driving reasons for my disorder in the first place.

The first day, I methodically inputted everything I would eat into a calorie counting app right as I woke up. It took me well over an hour, trying to decide how I'd plan it all out, knowing this amount would be so much more than anything I was ever used to. I convinced my mom to let me have a shot at this; to let me plan out my meals. I wanted to see if I was capable of this. She let me take control, and for the most part, I did well. About 2,000 calories into that first day, I saw just how exhausting Minnie Maud could be if I was not strategic about how much I ate. I felt uncomfortably bloated, overly full, and unsure if I'd make it all the way to 3,000 calories. I ended up eating protein bars and drinking whole milk mixed with protein powder to make it. This soon became a habit I relied on to gain the weight.

As I laid in bed that night, reflecting on the day, wondering how I could improve, I knew I'd have to face the foods that scared me most; anything with lots of calories and little volume. Coming from a diet that consisted of oatmeal, rice cakes, apples, and gallons of coffee, I was unsure how I'd make that transition.

Seeing it displayed in front of me made it a lot more real, but I also saw how I could make it work. The thought of eating 3,000 calories after months of eating only 10-20% of that is the epitome of daunting, but once I focused on calorically dense foods, it all became much easier.

There are a lot of much more nutritionally sound ways to recover from anorexia. I was not the healthiest in the slightest. My diet consisted mainly of chemically-laden protein bars, whey protein, peanut butter, pints of ice creams, and whole milk. After years of deprivation from sugary carbs, that's all my body wanted. Once I committed myself to Minnie Maud, I knew I had to go all in. I had to trust that my body would sort itself out, as the literature of Minnie Maud promised.

The only reason why I even lasted a week in Minnie Maud recovery, was that I promised myself I could always lose the weight again. Upon reflection, I know well enough this is not the right mentality. I used it as a safety net. It reminded me that this phase of life didn't have to be forever. If I found myself to be utterly miserable, I could always go back to how I used to be. Then, I reminded myself I was pretty miserable at the lower weight anyway. Not to mention, but everyone around me was also suffering a great deal. I might as well, I figured, see what this whole recovery thing was about. If I hated it more than the abysmal life I currently live, I could always give it up. No stress.

It took only a week or so for my body to adjust to the larger food intake. That both surprised and scared me. My biggest fear in jumping to 3,000 calories was that my body would find itself accustomed to that amount and then require it, even at what I deemed a safe and healthy weight. I, like many others who have ventured into Minnie Maud, worried that the scale would continue to rise, I'd lose control of my so-called "willpower," and I'd gain an exorbitant amount of weight. This caused me the most distress, but I calmed myself with the promise I could always restrict and lose the weight again. I wasn't fully committed to recovery, and keeping this idle, disordered thought in the back of my mind calmed me, helping me continue to trust in the process.

I journaled my food intake on Instagram. I posted every morsel on the account, documenting my emotions about the meal or snack, and giving myself the space to vent about the difficulties of this process—always feeling so large and out of control.

I felt extremely exhausted during this time. Part of Minnie Maud is giving up exercise entirely. In researching this method of recovery, this was the guideline I felt most reserved about. Exercise—running, mainly—was my release. It was the way I attained mental silence. It was the one time of day when I could completely shut away from disordered voices, or so I thought. In reality, the urge to run at the time was fuel purely by my disorder, but by doing so, I was given the peace of silence for an hour. I didn't know how I'd give that up. I figured I'd be fidgeting all the time, anxious and unable to sit still. However, eating 3,000 calories a day put my body into what was essentially hibernation mode.

Giving up exercise, for me, was less about the physical recovery my body required and more about breaking the disordered habit. Without question, I needed the time away from exercise to let me body physically heal; yes. That is true. I needed to understand what rest felt like.

However, giving up exercise during my weight restoration process was so much more about the mental reprieve. I needed to know what a full day of not exercising looked like. I needed to remember what sedentary felt like. At my worst, I spent over seven hours of my day moving my body in some sort of abusive away, stealing away whatever pockets of time I could. Almost all of that exercise was done in secret.

After several weeks of not exercising, eating well into the Minnie Maud guidelines, I experienced a feeling of clarity. I was not suddenly over the moon excited and content about not exercising, eating the largest quantity of food I'd ever tackled; all the while gaining weight at a rapid rate. I was, nonetheless, calmed by the notion of no longer living in secret. I didn't have to plan meals around when my parents were not home so I could convince them I ate more than the reality of my disorder. I didn't have to fake feeling unwell in order to slip away to my bedroom early in the night to parade around in loose pajamas huffing and puffing to various YouTube videos. Rather than scantily watching my parents during dinner, waiting for them to blink or look away just so I could shove the crust of my bread or a piece of chicken into my sock, I finally was able to eat like a normal human being.

Emotionally and mentally, my eating was not yet normal, but I could look around the dinner table and realize that on the surface, I fit right in.

That was a good feeling.

Christmas happened, and I had a bad day. The literal manifestation of the Grinch, one could have called me. I made Christmas seem like nothing to my family.

Scheduled to work all day, my parents preemptively planned a breakfast beforehand. They asked, walking on the eggshells I buried myself in. Resigned, I replied sure, yes we can have Christmas breakfast together. I laid the guilt on thick, making sure they knew how much something like that would burden me. I wanted them to know meals like that—out of structure, out of normal food—didn't suddenly become easy even though I'd upped my caloric intake.

Our conversation ahead of time concluded with the understanding that this family breakfast provoked mass anxiety in me. I pressed the point firmly: the first indication the meal itself actually might end in disaster. I laid down the ground rules, needing some form of control over this. I agreed to the family breakfast so long as there was adequate time for presents and eating the breakfast. I didn't ask for this because I was hell-bent on opening up the presents I'd received, but I knew if I felt even a moment rushed, I'd melt down.

Thanksgivings dramatics loomed in the forefront of my mind, and I teetered with terror at the thought of reconstructing a similar holiday disaster at Christmas. Together, the three of us came to the consensus that by 9:30 am, everyone was to be awake and out in the living room for presents. That allowed enough time for us to leisurely relax for almost two hours before I drove to work for the remainder of the day.

On Christmas day, I officially awoke at 7:30 am, restless from a night of picking at the folds of my blankets and scrolling through Instagram. I used to convince myself that browsing social media enticed drowsiness, though that is the farthest thing from the truth. I looked through pages and pages filled with gorgeous, decadent Christmas Eve feasts paired with walls of text expressing regret, sometimes bordering on hatred for the meals eaten by fellow people attempting recovery. Initially, I thought reading all of these shared experiences would calm my soul, quiet the disordered mind, but ultimately, it only hindered the strength I needed for the day lying ahead of me.

In evenings past similar to a night like that, the easiest solution was always to exercise. Running, my primary choice of activity, was a surefire way to turn everything else off. The worries, the fears, the trepidations, the trials; it all disappeared with the slow pitter-patter of my feet on the cement. With over a month into Minnie Maud, I knew my parents would never even consider the thought of me secretly exercising, so I easily could have made it out for a run. However, I made a promise to myself that I would not exercise.

To distract myself, I took my time curling my hair. As I wrapped sections of my hair around the iron, I breathed in and out, attempting to prepare for the day and the food. With so much to get through, I needed to relax if I had any chance. I turned Christmas music on. I watched the clock. I waited with the desperation for 9:30 to strike. The seconds ticked slower with each glance. It was as though I was a four-year-old waiting for her parents to wake up to see what Santa brought her, only with a pessimistic tone tacked on.

Before I knew it, my hair was formed into spirals, and I realized my stomach grumbled and grumbled. I suddenly felt *starving*, as though I'd gone a week without eating, not just a night. Oh, how the mind plays tricks when succumbed to mental illness. Hunger like that was a new experience for me. I didn't know how to react. Per

Minnie Maud guidelines, I needed to eat. That was the deal. That's what I signed up for.

But it was only 8:30. There was no way I was allowing myself to eat at that moment *and* in an hour with my family. Certainly, since Thanksgiving, I'd made progress, but I was not that strong. I brewed some tea and set out to journal, hoping that would help the time pass by.

9:30 came, and then, it went. 9:45 came, and then, it went. My family lazily came out of their caves around 9:55 and was greeted by an even more anxious version of myself. *But it is Christmas, Julia,* I pleaded with myself, *cut them some slack.* Nothing irritated me more than an unfollowed scheduled, but I channeled the parts of me that knew how to put on a show. I smiled, sighed to myself, smiled again, and let the small festivities begin.

We got through the presents. I spent the entire time watching the clock. I couldn't tell you a single present given or receive from that year. I couldn't tell you a passing phrase or note of conversation, either. Living in ad dead mind throughout the morning, I waited and waited for my dad to head into the kitchen to start breakfast, but it seemed as though no one cared to move forward with the morning.

Periodically, I left the room to put on a piece of my work uniform. My father, sensing my urgency, decided to save the rest of the presents, for when I came home for the night. Only a few remained, but the monster of myself needed her way.

He prepared his "donuts," which are biscuits lathered in butter and then later fried. Even though my mind prepared and calories counted, the layer of time pressure pushed me out of my comfort zone. Typically, everyone has three to four of these donuts, dipped or drenched in maple syrup, often paired with milk. I looked down at the communal bowl filled with the freshly baked,

warm and flaky biscuits, and sighed again. I couldn't do it.
Everyone at their normal amount, laughed and chatted. I
stared at my plate in silence, checking my watch, though I
knew the time and was counting the seconds already in my
head.

I ate one donut. My plate, sticky clean. I went
nowhere near the syrup or the milk. To top it off, I didn't
bring anything with me to eat for work. I went eight
additional hours with no food, no sustenance. When I
headed for the door, no one said goodbye or wished me an
easy shift. I knew I disappointed them. Though guilt
attempted to infiltrate me, I justified it by turning the
disappointment onto them in my head. It was their fault.
Not mine.

One biscuit was not enough to get me through the
shift, leaving me in an antsy, annoyed mood. With
Christmas being one of the busiest days for moviegoers,
the shift required me constantly running around, cleaning,
scooping popcorn, making banal conversations.

All throughout my shift, my annoyance at the
world shifted toward anger at my family, and then
ultimately toward my own attitude. I spent the work day
wishing I could change so many aspects of the morning.
Angered by my family's inability to stick to my plan, I
muttered in my thoughts over and over about how they
didn't care. They didn't understand me. They didn't even
try.

Midway through my shift, with all movies running,
the theatres slowed down. We had time to pause and rest
before the next swoop came in. I interacted with a few
customers who peered out of their movies for popcorn
refills. For the first time all day, I mindfully participated in
a conversation. A father brought his daughter out of the
movie, only minutes away from starting, because she'd
begged for an Icee. Watching the two of them interact,

bonding over slurping the icy drink, it pinged at me. The father thanked me with such grace and care. He told me he was grateful for working on a day meant for families. As he walked away with his sweet little girl in tow, I saw the image of myself and my dad growing up. Those moments of celebrating the early morning and surprising my brother and mom with donuts. It was the special memories like that, spontaneous, surrounded with food, that I'd missed out on for years at that point.

It was in that conversation with the father I realized I was the only thing wrong with Christmas. I was also the only thing wrong with Thanksgiving, I was the thing wrong, not anyone else. Everything had to be on my time. I was so selfish. I didn't even scoff at my poor attitude. My rationale at the time was; the entire morning would have run so much more smoothly had they all woken up on time. I always made it someone else's mistake. It could never be my fault. But I realized in those moments with the father and daughter getting a special movie treat, that my eating disorder was the only thing at fault.

Guilt crawled all over my skin, begging the clock to wind up faster, ending my shift to go home and make things right. I knew I couldn't. Not in a moment or in a conversation, but I wanted to make things right. I wanted to go back and change so many things about the morning; so many things about the year as well.

Of course, my family tried to understand. They were doing everything in their power to work around me and make it all better. The previous six months of their lives revolved entirely around my mood swings, my inability to eat meals, and their constant need to watch over me just to make sure I wouldn't kill myself. Yet there I was, defying the one holiday they asked for, the one morning they wanted to go well.

I took the laughter and fun away from Christmas morning. I caused the breakfast to feel rushed and awkward. I stole Christmas. I made it about me, when in reality, Christmas isn't about me at all. It is about shared memories and conversations and love and laughter and giving and charity. It's about slowing down and focusing on the people around me and the blessings of delicious food to cherish.

Eating disorders make you constantly think about you and yourself. What *you* are going to eat. What *you* are going to look like. What others think of *you*.

It was on this day that I saw how self-centered I was. I did not want to be. My thoughts, hijacked by a masked enemy, felt helpless. I went home and found that dinner was already eaten. They hadn't waited for me, and though this saddened me, what else could I expect? Typically, on days like that, I'd just make a safe meal; something with enough calories, but also, something that I felt completely comfortable with. In an attempt to make somewhat of amends as well as show them I actually was trying, I ate the same meal they'd eaten; a homemade pizza, practically impossible to calculate the calories. On top of that, I also had a pint of ice cream, knowing full well I'd a lot of calories to ingest if I was going to stick to Minnie Maud for the day. I knew I'd screwed up a lot, and if I wanted to progress forward in recovery, I needed to at least hit the 3,000 calorie minimum for the day. That was the last signal of fight for the day, the one thing that could make it better. With each bite, I destroyed the voices in my head, little by little, but I did not win at all on Christmas day.

My family didn't laud over me for doing any of this. They spoke to me and didn't hold anything against me, but they didn't praise me for choosing the pizza over a peanut butter and jelly sandwich or protein bars. They treated me as normal as they could. That's what they always tried to do. I didn't always let them, but they desperately wanted their normal healthy daughter back. They wanted the Julia they knew and loved, the Julia they knew I was capable of being. I wasn't there yet, but in that day, as I went to my room and prepared myself for sleep, I found a fit of anger within me that told me I could get better. I knew that Christmas day ended up as a weak day. But, I knew that if I pressed forward, I was capable of gaining strength, even on the weakest of days.

That night, I again had trouble falling asleep. I took to journaling and reflected on the hardest trials of my life. They are outlined in this book already. As I thought about them all, I realized that nothing, absolutely nothing, compared to the distrust of the mind. Anorexia by far was and is the greatest struggle of my life. No one understood. I felt more alone than ever. I stopped journaling and scrolled through Instagram. I posted my own meals from the day, explained the ups and downs of the day in massive paragraphs fit into small captions. There, I felt less alone. I felt more understood. I felt the unwavering hope of resonance. I felt like I had them, anonymous posters all over the world, and they also had me.

Because of them, I was going to gain the weight. I was going to get better. For my family, yes. For the people out there in the world who also struggled with eating disorders, yes. I was going to get better for them, too. I wasn't going to get better for myself. I knew I had to get better for myself if I wanted to go to college and get a fresh start, but that was forced. It was not voluntary. Getting better for myself never even crossed my mind as a true desire.

Lo and behold, I did. It required daily diligence, but the weight came back in about four months. I received college acceptance letters, and my parents wanted to talk about them. They wanted to talk about the future for me, whereas before they ignored the conversation. Now, their eyes lit up. We discussed and debated on which schools were the best option. I applied to many different schools, mainly in California. Ultimately, I decided San Diego State University was the college for me, and I began to plan my life. I'd forgotten what that felt like, planning.

In that final semester of high school, everything changed for me. I filled my life with activities. My theatre teacher cast me in a play. I attended school functions. I supported classmates' at sporting events. I rekindled friendships I thought I'd lost forever. I made the most of months I let fall to the wayside. I went to prom and ate the damn pasta dish without a second thought, only to go home and realize in the aftermath how profound that act actually was for me.

It was in those last months I realized just how much I failed at keeping a secret. I think I always knew that everyone was well aware of both my eating disorder and the social media documentation of it, but I liked naively convincing myself no one was the wiser. In fact, everyone knew. When people were able to steal me away for a moment of private connection, I was subject to conversations I didn't' know how to face. I constantly kept getting told I looked brighter.

"I feel brighter," I'd reply, unsure how to accept the compliment. "I feel like I'm actually living through my day, not just waiting for it to end."

That was the reply I always uttered. I didn't like the attention. It was all too kind, all too centered around the part of me I felt so much shame for. Just because I was making progress in my recovery had no effect on how much I despised the very idea of it being a part of my life.

Then, the conversations started to change. People started to pull me aside to tell me that they got me. That they, though to not to such a serious extent, had also had disordered eating behaviors. That they understood what it was like to feel like a stranger inhabiting someone else's body and hating every inch of the skin. Friends, even just mere acquaintances at the school started to pull me aside, not just to tell me how good I looked, but also to ask me questions. They either had a loved one in their life also going through the same thing, or they had the same thoughts pop up in themselves and wanted to know how to make it better.

I started to feel less alone. This time, not just online, but in the real world.

As I aged further and further away from my life revolving completely around recovery, Minnie Maud started to get a lot of flak. Credentials were called into question, as well as the validity of scientific research. At that point, I was far enough in my recovery, where I didn't necessarily feel compelled to worry about this, but I know for many others, this really hurt some progress.

Minnie Maud saved my life, therefore I cannot adequately criticize it. I acknowledge the many valid reasons to dislike and disagree with Minnie Maud. I will be the first person to openly admit that, in hindsight, I absolutely should have gone to a proper treatment center. I should have had doctors and therapists, but I stubbornly chose to do it on my own. Thankfully, it saved my life. I cannot help but be thankful for it, for stumbling onto the website in a heap of despair.

That all said, I am not a doctor. I did a decent amount of research, but I am the furthest from what one considers scientifically inclined. Minnie Maud made sense to me and my recovery experience, but I also recognize that it might not make sense to others out there. It worked for me. Read what you want from this. Find meaning in what you can. Take what you like and throw the rest out.

Because my experience is the only story I am capable of sharing, Minnie Maud is what I write about. I write praise for Minnie Maud not to diminish anyone else's treatments recoveries, but to shed light on what worked for me.

I do not believe Minnie Maud is the only way to recover. I don't even believe there is a "right way" to recover. I believe you have to do whatever the hell you can, fight tooth and nail, scratch at any molecule or recovery. Do whatever clicks in your head and run with it. Adjust as needed. Cry when you have to. Just recover. Just try. You have to.

Because of Minnie Maud, I gained the weight back I never was meant to lose. For me, it took four months to put about forty pounds on. At that point, my weight started to stabilize. After many conversations with my parents, they allowed me to start exercising again.

Minnie Maud is the method that helped me. Minnie Maud clicked for me. When someone is on death's door, debilitated by a starved brain, contrasting voices, and compulsive tendencies to harm oneself, do whatever is required to get better. Do whatever you can.

Recognizing trauma, trusting myself, and losing my virginity.

MY FIRST YEAR OF COLLEGE WAS the ultimate test. Though only two hours away from home, I wanted to treat it as if I was halfway across the world. I didn't want to use the fact that I could go home on weekends as an excuse to cling on to safety. I wanted to jump full force into this new aspect of my life and be Julia without the eating disorder. For the most part, I was quite successful. I tried to hide my eating disorder, but then I started to feel fraudulent. Eating wise, I was doing great. But I didn't feel like I was being as authentic and genuine with the people around me as I could and should have.

Rather than talking about my eating disorder and recovery online and on Instagram, I started talking about it in person. I felt capable of sharing my story without judging myself because I started to see no one else judged me for it. The pull I often felt to post my meals online faded away, dissipating while the urge to spend my meals with others surged.

Gradually, I gave up Instagram. It took a lot of me to do so, but even that alone made me see how much I relied on it.

Ultimately, my Instagram account both hindered and saved me. It turned what could have been a smoother recovery into something that still stuck with me for much longer. Had I not been so absorbed in scrolling, liking, commenting, posting, and participating, my mind would have had an easier time becoming occupied with more important things, such as establishing a community of friends and finding my family here in San Diego. I did make plenty of relationships, but just as I reflect, I know I could have done better.

To this day, though, I struggle staying in communication with everyone, even my family. A large portion of the reason *why this is* is because of my Instagram. It's not necessarily shame right now, but more so because I didn't want my eating disorder to act as a defining identity for me anymore. Though I am quick to boast about advocacy and forever and always will be the first one to talk about awareness, I am not blind to the fact that many people look at me with the first thing to come mind is, "anorexic."

Part of me makes that an excuse to shy away from cultivating strong and last friendships.

Instagram brought with it a fixation on certain behaviors and foods that were considered popular. I highly doubt my obsession with protein bars would ever had existed had I recovered outside of the online world. Since everyone else in the online community ate protein bars, I ate protein bars too. I played along. My eating disorder than manipulated this into a crutch, turning protein bars into safe foods, using any sneaky way to regain power.

The more I progressed into recovery, the more I saw how blurred lines became in the Instagram community. Those who posted captions with hashtags claiming intuitive eating also used the same hashtags I used with eating disorder recovery. Everything entangled, I started to understand that sometimes, there was no difference at all between the two.

There was also no way to tell who was truthful and who was putting on a front as a way to ahead in the never-ending competition for amassing followers and gaining popularity. Even now, by typing in #edrecovery to the search bar on Instagram, the top posts will yield and feature frail, white females who only give off the air of eating disorder recovery. I say this knowing there was a time when I was right there with them.

Though these individuals could very well be on their way to ultimately succeeding in recovery, many of them are years into maintaining this unhealthy, emaciated weight. It gives off a false perception to others about what an eating disorder looks like, further reinforcing the myths and stereotypes. I say this all with no intent of judgment, for I did it myself. I know firsthand how difficult it is to give up disordered behaviors that turned into creature comforts.

But, the more I strayed from my eating disorder and remained firm in recovery, the clearer I saw how unhealthy the recovery community on Instagram could be if I was not mindful of what I exposed my thoughts to.

That was how I made the decision to step away. I am so much better for it. I really am. I recognize and appreciate the place it had in my recovery—I truly do not think I would have made it out alive had I not had those people to identify with.

But, Instagram only had a place in my recovery. It only was one factor, it served a role. It was not my everything. It was not what could keep my recovery afloat. I had to say goodbye. That said, to this day, some of the best friends I cultivated in my life sprung out of commenting on each other's posts and supporting one another.

Giving up Instagram aided my relationship with exercise as well. I lingered all over the spectrum, going through periods of over-exercising and times, such as during Minnie Maud, when I did not exercise at all. With running, I have used and abused the movement. Whether it acted as mental silence or how I manifest my physical disappearance, years ago, I never utilized the exercises properly.

In early October of my freshman year, I was out at a party with several friends, one of which being my roommate. In a callous turn of phrase, my roommate made a rape joke. Not just a casual, *could-be-misconstrued-I-was-just-being-sensitive-get-over-yourself-Julia*, kind of rape joke, but a full-force rape joke.

Another girl who lived on the same floor as the pair of us walked by in a sheer shirt, exposing her breasts. Additionally, she wore a tight skirt that needed to be tugged down after every two or three steps.

"Look at her outfit," she started, garnering everyone's attention in the right direction as she whispered just low enough to not have the girl hear. With a giggle, she continued, "she's practically begging to be raped."

At the time, I'd never uttered even a slight confession to anyone as to what happened to me when I was fourteen years old, a freshman in high school. The closest I'd ever gotten was when I sobbed away in the principal's office just two weeks before graduation. It was a part of my life's narrative I was insistent on avoiding.

When she made that joke, my first reaction was to slap her. I didn't, but that's what my body wanted me to do on such a deep level. Mind you, I am not violent at all, but the anger she drew out from within my heart was unlike any other anger I'd felt toward another woman, especially one who, at the time, was a very close friend. Given that we were all only months into this transformative time of our lives, we all clung on to one another so quickly. I shared so much of my life with her in the hopes of becoming lifelong friends as everyone hopes for with roommates. Her joke stung, and I couldn't let it go.

Everyone else laughed. I looked around with furrowed brows and asked myself if I'd even heard what she said correctly. I tried to make excuses for her in those few seconds, but I knew I'd heard it right.

"Why on earth would you say that?" I said, with such force and hurt it surprised even myself.

"Julia, it was just a joke," my roommate replied, waving me away with the flick of the wrist. I knew she wasn't sober, but she also wasn't belligerent. There were no excuses. I pressed on, questioning her again.

"That's not funny. It's not funny at all. Do you really think she would deserve that?"

"Julia," she said, placing her hands on either side of me. She rested her palms on my shoulders, bringing her nose close to mine. "It's just a joke. Get over yourself."

She giggled again, kissed me on the cheek, and continued on to a different conversation. I stood there, stupefied. Within me I felt the urge to cry, but also to punch a wall. I made the stupid decision to walk home that night by myself and went to bed, confused at the spurt of emotions I found myself unable to control.

The following day at dinner, a group of us, my roommate again there, made plans to go out to another party. Fraternity parties bored me; jungle juice had more water than liquor, sweat drenched everyone, and it was always impossible to find the bathroom. However, I still didn't feel settled in college, nor had I found my niche or community, so I went with the crowd. I agreed to go out with them again for the night, but felt the least enthused I ever had been for a party.

Through a sporadic string of events, my roommate ended up leading the crowd out to the party while also leaving me and another girl behind, without notice. Classic mean-girl scenario, but honestly, it was the best thing that came out of my first year of college.

This other girl was Emily. Emily and I sat in our common area, doing the classic retaliation, griping about my roommate. We then dove into our own lives, chatting, sharing memories, and learning about one another. Finding ways to connect and finding ways to love one another. We stayed up until the early morning, eating cereal and watching *That's So Raven*. In that night, we went from strangers to best friends.

In between nostalgic episodes of childhood favorites, she brought up the rape joke from the evening before. She asked me if I felt personally violated by the joke. I looked at her, squinting my eyes, unsure how to respond. She looked at me with a grim smile, swished her lips to side and nodded her head.

"You know, you are safe with me." Emily said.

And then, she turned the next episode on. She didn't pursue the conversation further, and neither did I. But the following day at dinner, I suddenly felt emotions pull at me to tell her. Eating burritos together, I saw the picture before me: two friends, actively getting to know one another, and feeling very content with the friendship we were building. I thought back to Emily's words, her comfort of telling me I was safe, and I knew in those moments I was. I also knew I'd come so far in my recovery—I was eating a burrito for goodness sake—that this was a part of me I was holding back from healing.

"Can I tell you something that happened when I was in high school, and you tell me what you think about it?"

In an almost ceremonious fashion, she set down her burrito, clasped her hands together.

"Yes, please. Of course you can."

So, I told her everything. From the map of bruises, to the manipulative words, to the principal's office visit years after the fact. Emily sat there in silence, shoulders leaned in, eyes locked on me, absorbing every word.

When I finished, I asked, "Do you think what happened was wrong?"

At that, she sat back and gave me a look as though I'd just offended her entire genial line.

"Do I think what happened was wrong?" she retorted. "Julia, you were raped."

That was the first time I heard those words. She said them so loudly we both hunched over, realizing this was not the best conversation for public forum. We looked around, no one paid attention to us. She reached her hand over to my side of the table and gracefully grabbed my wrist.

"Julia, I am so sorry."

I shook my head.

"Thank you for letting me tell you." I said, very matter-of-fact, unable to tie emotions to the memories.

Giving those memories power happened because I kept it all a secret for so long. Because I'd never told anyone, I felt guilty. I felt like it was my fault. I let his words manipulate my own experience. I relied on what he told me rather than what actually happened. Giving voice to the violations made them, for the first time in my life, feel real. Not just a figment of my imagination. Even now, as I sit here and write this out, I often have to check my thoughts; just to make sure that I'm being honest. But I am. That's a symptom of the way he talked to me and made me do what he needed. I spent four years confused. I spent four years believing it was my fault, but in one conversation with a friend, that all changed for me.

The rest of my first year brought with it so much strength and growth. I talked about sexual assault in class. I was finally in courses where we navigate difficult topics. No longer burdened by the need to always talk about things through a Christian perspective (which isn't a bad thing, just a barrier of my high experience), students around me started to have intellectual, thoughtful debates about the physicality of our bodies. I learned about so many myths surrounding sexual abuse, and I even wrote about my experience for the first time.

During this time, I engaged in conversations a lot where people confided in me negative feelings they had about themselves. I spent so much time redirecting the thoughts and emotions over time, I realized I need to do this for myself. The honest comprehension and application of this was such a turn for my recovery.

College taught me a lot of things, but above all else, it gave me the power of critical thinking. Not just with academics, but about humanity and my own self-expression and worth. I got into the practice of recognizing negative thoughts that sent me down a darker path and revitalizing them into positive thought that boosted my morale and confidence.

For example, noticing that my body was bigger. Rather than lamenting my larger thighs and my forgotten thigh gap, I instead forced myself to celebrate this fact. The fact that I grew stronger and now had a healthy body that could carry me in this world much easier.

This was a process of fake-it-till-you-make-it, but when I took the time to actually refute the disordered thought, it eventually worked. If I started to praise myself for it having been hours since I last ate, I forced myself to stop; to tell myself that no that was not the right behavior or mindset. If I ever wanted to move past this, I had to get rid of these thoughts and recognize that they don't come from myself, but the worst part of me that somehow grew too much. Also, and I should mention that this when I was researching Minnie Maud, I told myself I could always lose the weight again. This is not the right mentality to have, but it acted as a safety net. My eating disorder was my default. Switching back was a comfort I knew I had saved in my back pocket. Secretly I savored this idea. A gift of sorts. One of the biggest pleasures was losing the weight in the first place, watching myself disappear day by day, forgotten meal after forgotten meal. Gaining weight gave me the chance to start over.

I convinced myself this was only a backup plan though. With a fake-it-till-I-make-it mentality, I attempted believing in recovery.

I stopped focusing on loving myself or hating myself. We are saturated with the self-love concept. People preach for it, promising it as the source of true health and joy. On the one hand, I get it. For years, I spent time and energy trying to hate myself into a version of me that I could love. That didn't work. However, I find myself asking people to love themselves in the midst of a messy, broken soul; an almost impossible task. One that results in feeling like a failure. It only makes the downward spiral deeper.

I started focusing on the tangible actions I could take that allowed me to become a more present, compassionate, diligent, and mindful human being. Someone people would enjoy interacting with. That shift in mindset alone allowed me immense growth. It required me to stop a lot of bad habits; wearing makeup that made me feel like a different person, declining dinner dates, and closing myself off from my own emotions. Since then, I reflect on every year, and I cry more and more every time. Not because life is worse, but because I'm allowing myself to actually express and validate the emotions within me. Sometimes, my emotions are irrational because, as I write this, I'm twenty-two and hormonal and going through lots of changes, but I don't second guess myself anymore. If I want to cry, I let myself. I always feel better when I do. This has made me feel the world around me a lot harder. But, I do feel like I'm existing and breathing and living through my days rather than just skating by.

At the end of my first year, I looked back on the year, amazed at the work I did and the community I built, but ultimately, so proud of how little I thought of food. The emotion of pride evoked within me was surreal, but I never wanted to let it go.

I returned for my sophomore year of college, fresh-faced, nineteen years old, with a new job, ready for an incredible year. Passed through all of the general education requirements, I was able to dive into true literature analyzation. Attending one the most liberal universities in the country meant that it was impossible to avoid the topic of sex in class. Especially as an English major at one of the most liberal universities in the country, students naturally want to discuss sex. Many of my peers came from similar backgrounds as me, where this was the first opportunity to openly discuss sex without judgment, so they went full force, and it seemed to enthuse professors. Regardless, I learned a lot: about the world, literature, and yes, about sex.

Everyone around me seemed sexually active, and it is impossible to dissect a novel in a literature course without someone bringing up the sexual nuances interwoven, like legs tangled in bedsheets. At the time, I was immersed in my studies, actively reading, creating, and writing. I wasn't particularly invested in seeking out a romantic partner, but it petered across my mind on occasion. No real interest settled within me, though.

One day after class, I had lunch with a few of my classmates. The conversation inevitably went toward the topic at hand when one of my friends, who I—to this day—greatly adore, made an offhand comment about me. We were in the midst of discussing various levels of attraction and how this played out in Vladimir Nabokov's novel,

Lolita. My friend was making a case that there are different levels of attraction, and not all are physical.

"Take Julia, for example," he said, gesturing toward me from across the table. I opened my eyes wide, already concerned for the next words to come out of his mouth. "She's not someone you want to have sex with."

Taken aback by this, all I mustered was, "What?"

My friend responded, "No. Julia. I mean, you're beautiful. You're just not the type of girl a man wants to be physically intimate with."

"Oh, okay," I said, a bit shell-shocked.

As soon as I could, I exited that lunch, not knowing how any of us were to recover from that. No one else seemed bothered by the exchange, and I'm not sure if that was because they too didn't know how to react or if I was just too sensitive.

I was only with guys during the conversation, so no one said anything, which, I get to a certain extent. I don't think I'd pipe in and say "oh, yes, you're very sexually attractive." That would come off wrong, too. There was no right way to swerve out of the comment, but I couldn't forget that it happened.

After that, I couldn't take my mind away from who I was as a sexual being. Did it not exist at all? Was I destined to not be that to anyone? I really didn't know. All of a sudden, I started thinking about sex more and more. Not in the sense that I was desperate to have sex, but I started to think about its meaning in life. I started to dream about attempting to have sex, only to find no one was interested in me. I wondered if I was labeled unattractive and there was something in my pheromones from being raped that made people not want to have sex with me. I wondered if sex was necessary for me. I didn't know if I needed it. I didn't know if I could enjoy it. I wondered if being raped meant I could never enjoy sex or if I'd ever be good at it because I wouldn't know how to separate sex from rape.

Then, in my creative writing course, I met someone. We shall call him Chad. Chad was cute and sweet, a year younger than me, but a wholesome, nice guy. He took me on two dates, both of which were nice. There is no other way to describe the time with him. He was nice. On our second date, I looked at him and thought, he is a sweet guy. He would treat me right. He seemed interested. We kissed, and it was nice. Nothing special. Nothing wrong either. Nothing was to come of us together, I was sure of that. I assumed he felt the same.

On our second date, we went out to a cliff site. Here in San Diego, checking out a cliff, overlooking the beach, particularly at sunset, is the epitome of what a stereotypical date is. Though nearing in on the month of May where spring tends to bring about a flourishment here in Southern California, the clouds bore in, proving the wind inherent by the sea stronger than either of us enjoyed. We stood around for a while, making half decent conversation, staring at the minor sunset viewable through the clouds. Eventually, we gave up and made our way back to campus. I was a resident advisor and he was a first-year student, so we both lived on campus.

Caught up in traffic, we again attempted to make conversation. We chatted about everything, from middle names, to favorite childhood memories, to future aspirations. I have always been one to dive deep and ask the important, vulnerable questions without much regard for social boundaries. Given the veracity and openness I cultivated on my blog, I thought that niceties were a waste of time. We are here on this earth to form connections and establish friendships. Anything else standing in the way of that is a waste of time. During that car ride, he told me about his own upbringing, and my heart went out to him.

Being from a broken home, I saw how he clearly experienced distrust in many of his former relationships and friendships. I saw the human in him. I looked at him again as we sat in the mist of foggy headlights, feeling the tension of every other driver around us, just wanting to be home. I looked at him, and again, thought to myself, he is a nice guy. He would treat me right. It may not be the most exciting thing in the world, but maybe, we could learn to love one another.

What should have taken fifteen minutes wound up taking us closer to an hour. As I stepped out of the car at the back entrance of my own building, I asked him if he wanted to come up. He said yes, and I sat back down in the car to wait with him while he parked. We climbed the stairs up to my room and put on a TV show, fooling no one that we'd actually sit down and watch the program. Before the theme song hinted at its tune, I'd slid into the nook of his arm, and we fooled around.

Enough time passed that Netflix went onto another episode, and we let the background noise fill the room. We broke away from pawing at each other to have a conversation about sex. I let him know I was a virgin, but I wasn't holding off for any particular reason. He didn't need to know the grimy details. He asked if I was comfortable moving forward, which I was. It lasted all of two minutes, during which all I recall is wondering how this could ever be so special that entire novels, poems, songs, and lives were defined by sexual prowess.

We are not here to discuss losing my virginity, but for some reason, it is here. For me, I know now that my eating disorder was so much more than my body's appearance. It was multifaceted, and one of the smallest links in the chain is about what I actually looked like. My eating disorder, for me, stemmed in the physicality of my body, the sensations, the treatment, the abilities my body retains. Even though I'd dabbled in intimacy with others, losing my virginity was a hurdle in my recovery. It was a sign that my past didn't need to define me, something I think a great deal about in all aspects of recovery. I needed to know that being raped didn't automatically set me off from the rest of the world. This boy didn't know I had been raped, and he likely never will. I didn't walk into that date even considering the idea of losing my virginity, but it subconsciously was always there.

The following day, I returned back to normal life. I told Emily what happened, but that was the extent of the excitement. My routine at the time was chock-full of work and school and finalizing everything before I set off for the summer. My study abroad trip to Spain was in the coming weeks, and the end of the year for a resident advisor is busier than ever. Combined with the standard assortment of final projects and exams, I knew there was no time in my life to cultivate this relationship with this boy. I knew I couldn't make him a priority.

With grace, I ended things with him. He didn't take it well. I hurt him. I hurt him a lot. I never anticipated the emotions he felt for me had grown so strong already. I did my best to let him down easily. I had never been put in that position before. Looking back, I want to say I did all the right things; we had an open dialogue where I explained my emotions and where I was at in life. I thought he understood. We left the conversation on good terms.

Let's fast forward to the concluding week of school. As mentioned, I met this boy in a creative writing course. The latter half of the semester, each of us took turns reading aloud a five page short story we wrote for the class. Then, our peers would critique in a somatic seminar session.

When this boy's turn came, he stood up to the plate, ready. He shuffled his papers on the table and set out to read. For these readings, the class rearranged the desks into a circle. As though he planned for this, he sat directly across from me. Then, he set off to read a story that haunts me every day.

His story was simple: boy meets girl. The girl's name: Kathleen. My middle name. Hmmm, I remember thinking as I sat there, reading along on my own copy. That didn't sound right. Unsettlement washed over me. The story he wrote recreated everything; our date, getting stuck in a backlog of cars on the freeway, leading up to us having sex. Everything was respectful until the moment when the two characters walked into the girl's bedroom.

He then ripped me apart, mentioning the girl's figure as that of a, "pasty, ugly body of a twelve-year-old boy." How it took all of his gusto just to get erect. It continued on an on, only getting more vulgar, and more hurtful. When he finished his story, he looked up, smirked, and then winked at me. Everything he'd written was specifically and intentionally meant to hurt me.

All of my classmates were none the wiser. No one knew we had been out on a few dates. They critiqued it as though it was a pathetic attempt at odd erotica. No one liked the story, but he didn't care. That wasn't the point of him writing the story. His words were written only to hurt me. And that he did so successfully. I just had to sit there and take it too, because what on earth could I say? If I said anything, I would be outed.

That was the end of it. Every so often I'd see him on campus, but we never spoke, we never even made eye contact. I supposed you can look back on this and come to the conclusion that I used this boy; perhaps I did. We both hurt each other at the end of it all.

So why is this here? Why am I taking the time to write about this? Am I doing it out of retaliation? To get the final word? No. I don't think so. Otherwise, I'd use his actual name.

Losing my virginity was a pivotal point in my recovery. The aftermath of losing my virginity? Even more.

Physicality, for me, has always been so entwined with my mentality. When people hurt me through the means of my body, it screws with my mind. Enduring this instantly made me want to warp myself into something more pleasant or something I could disappear to. That's the dichotomy of this narrative in my story.

Essentially, he wrote out what I previously aspired to be. I wanted to have the body of someone who was pale and frail. He wrote that. I accomplished that. It brought me no happiness. My eating disorder was never about my looks. My eating disorder became about vanity only when others based my value on vanity. After not feeling valued for so long, I grasped onto anything that did bring me meaning. Some people saw that in vanity, but for me, it brought no happiness. Instead, I wound up just worse off than before. So, I got better. I worked so hard to get better. At the same time, though, his story brought with it massive shame as I sat there, watching others crying and smile with bits of laughter at the story.

This boy made me question everything about my recovery or whether I'd truly recovered at all.

Sometimes you do it for yourself, and sometimes you do it for others.

HALFWAY THROUGH COLLEGE, I studied abroad in a small, coastal town in the south of Spain, Valencia. It was a summer program focusing on English literature and Spanish speaking. At that point, I'd already taken well over a decade of Spanish courses, and while intellectually I considered myself verbose, the ability to conjugate and converse in real time left me frozen. Throwing myself into the mix, I felt at the point, would be the only way for me to jump from understanding the language to actually using it.

Traveling in recovery, previously, was hit or miss, rocky waters, a, "let's see how this goes." Often, there were other dynamics at play, navigating familial relationships, feeling watched at meals, monitoring my activity of the day. Mainly though, it was the feeling watched aspect. Before I studied abroad, I only traveled with people, mainly my family, who knew my story. They knew I had an eating disorder. Only people I find myself holistically comfortable with are those I don't set out to prove anything to. With my family, while I love them, endearingly so, I can't honestly say I feel comfortable in my recovery around them. Because they saw every ounce of my deepest months of struggle, I know they are bruised and battered by it. I have no doubt they love me, but ultimately I know they look at me and question where I am at and if I'm fooling them or if I'm really fine.

When I arrived at the airport, I observed the other students. Twenty-seven of us in total, and not a single face I could call by name. There was one girl who had a face I recognized from the gym, but I did not know the first thing about her. It was in that moment that, like my first day of college, I realized how beautiful it was to be alone here. Not lonely, as I saw the faces of potential friends all around me, but alone in the sense of my story was mine to know solely. Absolutely any of these peers of mine could somehow find a way to look me up online and find out who I was, but I knew no one cares that much to do that.

As we made our way around introducing ourselves to one another, it was a serene, healing moment to say, "I'm Julia," and end the sentence there. No, "I am Julia and I have anorexia, but I'm working on it." No, "I'm Julia, and I feel really good about my recovery but I can't lie, I'm really terrified about studying abroad because of all the unknown food." It was just, "I am Julia," and that felt so dang liberating. I didn't set myself up with any expectations of failing myself. I didn't let that even come up, because I refused to let that exist in my identity while studying abroad.

When I moved to San Diego for school, I was only two hours away from my family. To me, this distance classified as far enough where I am definitely away, but close enough where I had the ability to go home if necessary. There, while a sense of freedom layered over my lifestyle, I knew I still had my parents nearby watching out for me. Here in Spain, I was on my own. Especially once I made the decision to forgo disclosing my eating disorder on any medical documents (one twisted benefit of not having a proper diagnosis, I guess?), I knew my time in Spain would ultimately indicate my actual recovery progress thus far.

I knew, going into the trip, that I'd experience basically any and all stressor that like to turn my disordered thoughts and behaviors on. All of my routines; gone. Moving to Spain was a fresh start, making those first few meals and days crucial.

On the plane ride over there, I didn't sleep. Instead, I witnessed a full night in passing. I tangled my laptop toward the window as to not disturb any of the other passengers, and I took the hours to describe every intricate detail of the night trailing along. I look back on that writing and find it so particularly mundane. It is a testament to the desperate need I had to take my mind off the impending summer ahead. It was in those hours the sheer gravity of my decision to study abroad hit me. Always before that, throughout the entire application progress, it was a vague idea of travel. I began to cry, not out of terror or regret though, out of hope. I pleaded with myself. The words on my screen turned from crater descriptions to prayers of resilience. I wanted to do the trip right. If this time abroad ended up as a failure, I could blame no one but myself. I had to do this right for myself. I deserved to give myself that fighting chance. I wanted this summer to define my future.

When I stepped off the airplane, I viewed this as the inciting action of my storybook trip to Spain. This was the movie scene magic, where I leave all my irrational troubles back in California and gallivant across Europe. Hope engulfed me.

I don't whether my naiveté was at an all-time high or if I truly just let a manipulative part of my mind take over.

My time in Spain was earth-shattering, life-altering, and peacemaking. But it also made my idea of recovery much more complex than I ever anticipated. No matter what I told myself or how diligently I worked, I couldn't pretend that crossing international borders suddenly gave me a new perspective on the toxic anorexic mindset ingrained in me. That said, I was at a stable point in my recovery. I knew the amount of food and calories my body needed to feel nourished and satisfied throughout the day.

Choosing to eat was no longer an hour-long battle but rather a five-minute check-in with my body asking it, "Hey girl, what do you need and want right now? Are you okay?" Under my belt, I already incurred two years of recovery. I knew I took with me tools to keep myself accountable. I didn't have any worry about a full-on relapse, but I was well aware my anxiety with food would go far up.

When it came to food, my strategy was to watch the others around me, monitor how much they ate, when they went back for seconds, and when they left food on the plate. This, coupled with honoring my hunger cues, felt like a strong mechanism for keeping my weight in check. At the time, I thought this was the right decision. Only now can I reflect and see this likely came from a corner of the mind that needed to give into disordered thoughts a bit. While in the midst of it, I justified my observances as ensuring I ate enough, I look back now and see I was doing this to safeguard my daily intake. I ate *only as* much as the other girls ate, and never more. Even still, my time in Spain broke the rigidity I struggled with back in the United States. Here in America, I have the great luxury and privilege of choosing almost all of my meals. Additionally, because I spent years researching the calorie contents of basically all American food, I was and still am an expert on estimating the nutritional content of meals. But in Spain, I did not know where to begin. The nice thing about that was I could not even beat myself up for it because I didn't have the choice. This relinquished any desire or urge I had to control my meals.

Spain's way of life is the antithesis to life in the United States; laidback, focused on lingering, leisure, playful chatter and interpersonal communication, appreciating life for what it is by enjoying the simple pleasures in front of you. Everything in Spain took an hour longer than I expected it to, but it was okay. What was expected of me was afternoon naps, sleeping in hours later than my normal routine, and meandering over meals for hours on end.

At a certain point during my time in Spain, I felt *good*, but I also felt alone. There I was, crafting these intense, quick, loving friendships, but I was leaving out an entire integral part of how I became the person I was lying on the beach with these adventurous other students. One day, I blurted it out to my closest friend on the trip Luis. I gave him the link to my blog. He asked questions. I explained as best as I could. He didn't judge me. Connecting with him, confiding in him, though he couldn't directly relate, opened the door to a level of vulnerability that sealed this summer program off as easily the best experience of my life thus far. I was purely and wholly me and curated a life around me I was proud of.

During the trip, I also learned what it meant to be kind to myself. Back at college, I was constantly absorbed with the guilt of not conforming to the party culture. There in Spain, I learned. I could not be true to my health and wellbeing by going out every night. That was not how I imagined enjoying other cultures. It was one chapter of it, to be sure, but I needed every other part as well. That meant choosing to sleep early and watch the sunset on the beach most days, because that is where I saw a corner of the world that broke me and brought me to this deeper appreciation of the sheer beauty in this world I took for granted during the depths of my eating disorder.

Spain was a rush of odors, food, language, alcohol, sand, touching, and embracing. Ham everywhere. I saw life outside of my own. Knowing that there are such a large number of different types of people, types of beauty, and types of joy, aided me in becoming comfortable in my own skin, in my own beauty, and in my own joy. I learned that the limit on my world experience was self-imposed because once you're there, the world is ready for you. I ate the most decadent paella and swam in pitchers of sangria. I full sunk into the immersion, learning to try the food without dissecting every ingredient in it. I learned that I loved rice. Not just enjoyed it, but *loved* it.

The whole experience exhilarated me. I could talk about my recovery for hours on end, but nothing challenged me more and succeeded in freeing me from my comfort zone like moving to Spain.

In Madrid and Barcelona, I could walk up to practically anyone and stammer out a few words in Spanish before transitioning into English and they would respond back in English. In Valencia, though, the locals didn't have it. They forced me to try and fail through my broken Spanish. Those first few weeks, I felt a lingering wave of humiliation every time I wanted to ask what street I was on. Then, I realized that everyone who I spoke with was actually remarkably kind. Sure, they forced me to speak Spanish, but of course. As they should have! I was in their country, on their turf, in their land; there for the pure purpose of immersing myself in their culture. I had to suck it up. Once I made that switch, it was as though a new dimension of the world unlocked for me. I stepped through this barrier I didn't even know was plastered in front of me.

One day, in particular, left a lasting impression on me. Students from different programs from all over the world packed into a bus, with many of us sitting on the floor in the aisles or piled on each other's laps. We were all soaked with sweat, but the excitement and conversation consumed us all, leaving us without a bother. I briefly had met several of the other students at a local bar a few days prior when we agglomerated together to watch a World Cup match between Spain and Italy. We were en route to

Albufera, about twenty-five minutes south of Valencia.
Albufera is rich with dunes, beaches, rice fields, and most
notably; the largest lake in the country to explore on a boat.

Surrounding the calm water, a swampy marsh
encircles everything, reminiscent of parts of Florida,
humidity and all. Piling onto traditional fishing boats
stocked with umbrellas, we enjoyed a time of serenity,
participating in little conversations, and taking pictures,
and watching the view. It was stunning.

Following the boat tour, we took a few minutes to
grab a beer, eat a tapa or two, before making our way to
the second destination of the day, one we all anticipated
since we landed in Valencia: Toni Montoliu. We had a
paella cooking class on the agenda. Initially, I expected the
whole activity to last maybe two hours, foolish as I was. I
had no idea what I was in for, and my, oh my, was I
delightfully surprised.

The man himself gave us a lengthy tour of the
property showing us all of the small details that make his
food special. Everything is grown on the property, and we
learned about the process and the great care he takes with
his food. The way he and his family on the property
approached food and nourishment was an entirely foreign
concept to me, but one I desperately wanted to grasp onto.
He truly looked to his food as a gift, one of which capable
of expressing every emotion, love, passion, exhilaration.
Knowing I was in for a feast, I realized I suddenly had no
anxiety. Having the community of a calm and safe space to
enjoy the food changed everything for me. I was actually
excited.

Dogs and kittens roamed about the entire property,
sneaking up to snag some love by ramming into my calves.
I always relinquished and squatted down to scoop them up
and carry them around for as long as they let me. Donkeys,
horse, goats, rabbits, and chickens also approached me

without fear. It suddenly made me question how separated we are in America from animals, both in terms of food and companionship.

Just beyond the livestock stood rows and rows of fresh vegetation. Here, he told us all to go out and pick fresh tomatoes for our paella dish. I was amazed; not only did Toni Montoliu trust us young, silly strangers to pick apart his field, but he encouraged us to take our time searching and searching to find the absolute perfect tomatoes. Yanking a juicy stem off the vine himself, he squeezed it lightly, took one waft of it, and bit in voraciously. "It's a connection you feel when it's right," he said, "Allow yourself to, for once in your life young Americanos, to feel connected to the world."

I'll never forget those words. Toni Montoliu spared no indulgence for us, and picking the tomatoes was only the first experience of the day. We picked out green beans, onions, we scooped out the rice. With vegetables picked and ingredients prepared, the cooking began. Cooking paella is a timely ordeal, and everyone took some time in the kitchen. While others learned the tricks, stirring the large skillets, I sat on a horse-drawn carriage with friends I made only hours before, perched atop an unstable wooden contraption sipping on fresh sangria, fanning away the saturated heat. In my ever-improving Spanish, I spoke to one of the women that lived on the property about writing and literature, and she shared with me a Spanish poem she memorized. She taught it to me and we laughed as I failed and failed again miserably, but ultimately I got it. She kissed me on the mouth and knocked her forehead and against mine and whispered to me, "Ave incipiente, estoy orgulloso de ti." *Budding bird, I'm proud of you.*

When the paella neared full preparation, Toni Montoliu called people one by one to taste test the broth. It required every person's approval, he told us, otherwise he'd work until not everyone was satisfied, but until everyone was ecstatic. He treated us like sheer royalty. As each person, slurped their spoon, I watched him scan his or her eyes, awaiting the response. Toni Montoliu is a man who unconditionally adores his job. He performs his passion every day. I admire him, and I swore that day I'd be that kind of human myself.

The meal itself overwhelmed me. Course after course, ten in total. Loaves of bread, breaking apart with flakes amassing on the table as we tore off bits. Fresh white bean hummus, ground from the land, slathered on more bread, a sweeter sort. There was Valencian salad, bravas, deep fried potatoes soaked in olive oil and garlic, pimiento, mussels, three different types of paella, rabbit, escargot, caramelized pumpkins, juicy, sweet, dripping melons, and a different liquor for every dish. I stuffed myself silly. I tried everything and shut off any voice in my head. I realized halfway through the meal that mind was quiet. The initial thoughts vanquished and there I was, in this little town halfway around the world, drowning in a feast, yet still able to breathe and smile.

Toward the end of the meal, Toni Montoliu came over to me and few of the other girls at the table, asking, "*¿Estás listo para cantar para nosotros?*" Most of the girls laughed him off, politely declining, but all of a sudden, I stood up. I grabbed the microphone from him and he led me over to the karaoke machine. Quickly scrolling, I found my cliché, perfect karaoke song, "Don't Stop Believin'" and belted it out like my voice would leave my body tomorrow if I didn't use it today. By the time I made it to the chorus, many of my friends popped up with me and echoed the tune. Halfway through the song, my professor came over and took the lead much to my utter excitement, while I hit the dance floor with everyone else and spun and spun and spun.

At the time, I blamed my behavior on the tequila, and while I'm sure that was a factor, I knew that somewhere in me, this felt good and right and powerful and like something I always wanted to ability to just stand up and do. I wanted to look out into a crowd and be my authentic, carefree self. This moment was the first one in years when I even realized that part of my soul still existed. On that dance floor, I spent the next hour twirling away, and swaying to the renditions of all of these stranger's songs. My professor got back up to perform a whole Red Hot Chili Peppers concert, and I finally plopped down into a seat from the exhaustion and the satisfaction of the feast. I looked around and saw how free everyone was—how free I felt myself. There were no boundaries between me and the world. I didn't care how I presented myself. I was just me. I just lived and enjoyed.

Every day in Spain was exhilarating. All thoughts of the blazing heat, the dehydration, the scraggly soreness of my legs; it all dissipated. In Spain, the clock was a nuisance, an added, artificial, unnecessary cause of stress. They shrug it off. With that first breath I inhaled stepping into the country. My time in Spain was quaint and quiet, yet every night I shuffled into my stiff dormitory bed, at the turn of an all-too-late hour, utterly exhausted, with a warm heart, full belly, and the trace of my lingering smile calming me to sleep.

When I arrived home, I was not at all prepared for the cultural shock. I did better upon my arrival in Spain than I did upon my return home. I cried for days on end, and I instantly started planning a new trip abroad. It was the only way I could get myself out of the emotional hole I dug on my flight home. I had to remind myself the only obstacle between me and Spain was another plane ticket.

Coming back from Spain, I looked into a mirror, and for the first time in months, I examined my figure. Part of me knows I purposely never took the time to look at myself in the mirror while I was in Spain because I knew I was losing weight. I never actually admitted that to myself while I was over there, but I know that is exactly what I was doing. I made so many mental strides while in Spain, but I simply wasn't eating enough. Recovery is a compilation of ten thousand little aspects of living, but one of the main tenets is eating enough. Trying sangria, paella, and all of the different tapas at local bars granted me access into a new realm of recovery by the adventurous soul in me returning, but recovery meant nothing if I let myself slip into an unhealthy weight again.

At that point, I wasn't tied to the scale as I used to be. It still was on my mind, and I knew how I much I was supposed to weigh. A friend of mine picked me up from the airport, and I stayed at her house overnight. I slept on a blowup mattress in her kitchen. While attempting to sleep, I became viscerally aware of the mass quantity of food surrounding me. Instinctively, I wanted to snoop through her pantry. It was a habit of mine I'd forgotten about, only let loose when I was truly and actively in starvation mode. I used to evaluate every product sitting in someone's pantry when they were not around, even food I had no interest in ever eating. Scanning the nutrition label, I'd memorize serving sizes, caloric content, grams of sugar, and so on. Then, I'd neatly place it in the exact position I found it, never to be found out. It's how I accrued my colossal database.

Minutes passed, on and on, as I played the mental battle of deciding whether or not to peek through. I knew it was not something someone in recovery should do, but I went through all of the motions, trying to find some which way to rationalize the behavior. Was I hungry? Yes and no. I was hungry. I didn't want to eat, though. That, in and of itself, should have been the first of many red flags to me, but the jet lag coupled with the sadness I felt already missing Spain, my mind wasn't strong enough to recognize any of the warning signs. Not that I make any excuses.

Next question: If my friend came out, would I feel ashamed? Yes and no. Yes, because I already knew I should not be poking around her pantry at 12:30 in the morning while she has a sleeping baby in the next room. No, because I already had my excuse. I simply could reply that my body was used to eating at different times and I felt like I needed a snack to tide me over for sleep. Again, this clearly should have set my own recovery mind off. I thought nothing of it.

Final question: Should I eat? Yes and no. Yes, of course I should. Though I'd not stepped on the scale, I knew I could afford to have an extra snack or two. No, because I didn't want to eat.

I peered over at the clock again, by the time I sat up from the blow-up mattress, it was 1:45 in the morning. *That's it*, I thought to myself, *if I don't get up right now, I'll think about it for another hour and lose any chance at quality sleep. I'll make myself a snack, I will*, I thought to myself. Eating something will completely shut off this roundabout of meaningless thoughts and urges.

For over an hour, I methodically touched every granola bar, pasta sauce jar, and carton of juice. Fifteen minutes in, I realized I wasn't looking to acquire new information, but to test myself. Calorie counting was impossible in Spain, hardly anything I ate came from a package, and even rarer did I prepare my food for myself. I didn't even realize why I played the game in the first place—I wanted to make sure I hadn't lost my mental stamina for knowing nutritional information. My eating disorder quickly reminded me it existed here in America.

In the morning, I stepped into her bathroom and saw a scale lying on the cold tiled floor. With no one else awake, I saw it as my opportunity to hop on the scale and observe the damage I'd done. Sure enough, I'd lost a whopping 16 pounds. Even had I been at a weight where I could have lost 16 pounds and still been considered a medically healthy weight, I was *not* in Spain long enough for anyone to lose 16 pounds in a healthy manner. I was actually horrified at the number.

I looked at myself in the mirror and took in every inch of my body. I made a mental note of where the bones protruded, how flat my stomach was, the slimming angles of my thighs. My eyes made their way back up to my face, and I sighed. I loved this body. I loved how I looked. I look back at pictures of this time even now and crave this body, even as I know it was not healthy for me. Even now, I want that body back. I felt so defeated. I was miserable being back from Spain, but here was an unexpected gift: I loved the tiny body I came back with. I remember thinking it was my best souvenir.

Then, sensing that I was about to burst into tears in the middle of my friend's bathroom in her tiny apartment while she has a one-year-old sleeping mere feet away, I made my escape. I threw on a sports bra, running shorts, and sneakers, and bounced out of the house, making my way toward my old running route from when she and I were neighbors. I cried the entire time, and I was also too exhausted from the jet lag to run farther than a quarter of a mile. I ended up sitting in front of someone's house, perched on their lawn, sobbing at myself. Dry, tearless cries. I was so angry with myself. Best souvenir? An emaciated body was my best souvenir? Not the daily memories of adventure and exploration. Not the countless friends I made? Not the passion for diversity?

I hated myself more in this moment than I had in years. I didn't deserve any of it. I didn't deserve the trip. I didn't deserve the weight I'd lost. I didn't deserve to have any of the memories or even the chance to return to Spain one day.

I sucked it up, stopped crying, and went back to my friend's house where she had breakfast waiting. Clearly, I was not going to make it through any interaction with people who knew me without them being on red alert for a relapse. I could already tell she was worried about me. Not wanting to put up a fight, I ate the food and smiled through the lies of sharing in my happiness with her. I couldn't describe to her or to anyone else the despair I felt upon returning to America. In one of the info sessions prior to leaving, the counselors made it clear that students struggle after returning from their time abroad because the exhilaration one feels being on there own for the first time is inexplicably rare and pure.

In reality, the majority of students who have the opportunity to study abroad—let alone attend university in the first place—are upper middle class and above. Being so, this also tends to lead to the assumption that these same students lived very sheltered lives. I know that I did. The minute I left the country and went abroad on my own, knowing I was responsible for myself fully, that was when I knew recovery was actually something I had to hold onto. I knew my time abroad was my chance at learning what life meant and what living was supposed to feel like.

I felt that with each breath I took in Spain. America suffocated me where in Spain, I felt liberated.

For a month, I did nothing to change my weight. My parents, though I lived with them for a few weeks and I'm sure they noticed, did nothing, either. Not once did they bring it up to me. I don't know if they truly didn't see it, or if they felt as though they were at the point where they couldn't change me. For whatever reason, I didn't mind either way. I enjoyed this. I didn't take the time to try to heal because I mourned my time abroad.

On a run a few weeks after my return to California, I put on a podcast aimed toward fellow women in recovery from anorexia, and orthorexia. The guest interviewed made this same overrun claim, "I learned I needed to love myself before I was able to love another."

The following day, I moved back to San Diego for my second year as a resident advisor. If you're unfamiliar with the job, essentially a resident advisor lives with first-year students in the residence halls, acting as their advocate, mentor, friend, and often, their babysitter. I loved my job for a plethora of reasons, and it was a bright spot in returning to San Diego. I felt fulfilled in this position, knowing I was easing the transition for many students coming into a scary, exhilarating new season of life.

For my residence hall, a floor consisted of around sixty-five students. Knowing that is a large quantity, the college set it up to have two resident advisors per floor. I would be set up with a co-resident advisor.

Enter: Ian.

Ian came into my life, whether I wanted him or not. Knowing I needed to establish a friendly rapport with the coworker I'd collaborate with the most, I shot over to his room the minute I heard his door open. The space between us mere yards, I hopped over, padding my bare feet on the striped carpet. I turned the corner and knocked on his door, cheerily singing his name. I knew his name and gathered enough familiarity of his looks based on his Facebook profile picture to hope we'd get along.

When the door opened, it was his mother. She let me know Ian was down at the car grabbing a few more of his items, and we chatted lightly until he arrived. A few minutes later, the elevator opened, greeting me with the presence of an older, burly man, followed by his son, the one who soon came to be the most important person in my life.

I couldn't help but laugh at the slight, curly-haired frenzy of a boy, growing into the man he always knew he could be, as he carried a television the width of his arms, covered with a blanket undoubtedly made by a girlfriend from his in high school. Blind to the world, covered by the electronic in front of him, his mom called out, "Ian, the other RA is here to meet you."

With a sudden, almost ferocious thump, he dropped the television to the floor and gave me a bear hug, letting me know how stoked he was to work with me. Immediately, I knew he'd be someone I'd have to keep at arm's length; the eagerness overwhelmed me. I, still aghast at the fact I was no longer studying abroad and gallivanting along the Mediterranean (pathetic and trivial and I know I sound like a brat, I realize I completely was for the time), had no interest in cultivating any new friendships. With him, I knew I'd need to walk a fine balance; otherwise, I'd end up in something I wouldn't know how to get out of. Still, he was kind, and funny, and charismatic, and tried to make me smile from the moment I met him.

I did everything in my power to push him away, to make him a coworker and nothing else. However, his charisma and charm prevented any of my pushback from actually following through. Given the sensitive nature of our job, he learned of my past very quickly on. The first two weeks of the job, we sat through different training sessions, each dealing with the horrific realities of our job we might have to face, including but not limited to: suicidal ideation, sexual assaults (utterly and disgustingly rampant on college campuses), and eating disorders, to name a few. After each session, the various residences halls would separate and go to their own buildings to have a debriefing session.

Sensitive to many of the topics, I often found fault with the rhetoric used in each of these particular situations, seeing as though I knew first hand some of the terminology used on me was not at all helpful. Ian knew straight away that I was a damaged soul. Still, he didn't run away. Instead, he asked questions. He wanted to know about me. He thought highly of me. He told me how proud he was of me. I'd had that said to me before, but not by someone who expressed romantic interest in me. Ian looked at me with so much confidence in who I was in an individual. He helped break me out of twenty years of insecurity. After having the same destructive thought patterns reinforced and repeated over and over and over, he saw something different in me.

I attempted to resist, but he only persisted. One night, I sat on the loveseat in his room, as he stood over his large wall calendar.

"How much time do you need?" he asked with a sly grin on his face. "When can I take you out on a date?"

We went back and forth bartering and compromising. We finally settled on a date in the near future. It was a jovial, light-hearted conversation. The room filled with the fumes of his open expo marker. He'd write down a heart on a date, and I'd walk over and wipe it away with my finger. We laughed and laughed. My resistance weakening by the minute. No one ever made me laugh like he did.

"You don't know what you're getting yourself into," I said to him.

"Let me see."

"You won't like me. You'll regret all of this."

"Try me."

"I am not easy."

"I don't need easy."

I looked at him. His puffy curled locks squashed by his favorite hat pulled backwards. I studied him. He looked sad, but hopeful.

"I get it." He started, shrugging his shoulders, hands open to the world. "You have gone through so much. I cannot even begin to imagine what it was like to battle through all you went through. But, I want to spend time trying to know, trying to understand." He closed off the expo marker and took a seat next to me.

"I don't know if I'm capable of being a happy girlfriend for you. That's what you deserve."

"Relationships aren't meant to be perfect and rosy all the time. We will have hard times. That's life. But it doesn't mean we give up. It means we talk and we try, and we work through it. If you and I work, we have to promise we won't give up."

As he said these words to me, I found myself holding back tears. No one ever had spoken to me like that, especially someone who had met me only weeks before. I shook my head, giving him the quietest of a yes with my gesture. I stood up, drew a heart around a date for the following week, much earlier than he had hoped for, and wished him a good night. Two days later, I kissed him; I could not even wait for the date.

Within a month, our relationship became full-fledged. We informed our supervisor, we posted on social media, we gushed about one another to our friends. The more time spent with Ian, the more I laughed. The more I smiled. He taught me to loosen up and just enjoy life. Neither of us focused much on school or work during our first year together; instead, we explored the city, watched movies, and learned about the lives we led that ended us there together, utterly interwoven.

It feels bleak to admit this now, writing it all down in the aftermath of our breakup, knowing I chose to walk away from him. I have never met anyone like Ian. I have never met anyone who made me feel loved in the unique way Ian did.

All things and people came alive in his company. Seeing the world through his eyes made all colors sharper, deeper, and brighter. His merry warmth brought a new voice of laughter in me. Life felt joyous and light around him. I gave up on the incessant worrying I plagued myself with. Through him, I realized that my eating disorder served a purpose in my life I never actually saw. The traumas I endured made me feel heavy. My brain, existing as best as it could on a malnourished level of intelligence, attempted to eradicate the problem by losing weight. I took the trauma as a physical manifestation of burdening weight when all along it was emotional and mental weight dragging me through hell. Constantly being in Ian's presence allowed me to see this for the first time. Living a life in which I thrived had nothing to do with how much I weighed. I could disappear completely, weighing nothing, but the pain would still exist. I had to fill my life with what brought me joy; Ian helped me do this. He saw so much in me, when all I saw was someone who failed repeatedly.

One of the things about myself I've learned in recovery is that I feel safe with people when I am comfortable eating around them. The minute I can fully enjoy a meal with someone, I have it set in my heart that I care about them and want them in my life. Eating, for me, is such a personal, vulnerable position I set myself in, that to do so in front of someone requires more mental strength. Having come back from Spain where such a large importance was placed on communal gatherings centered on food, I had the benefit of transferring this over to my relationship with Ian.

Soon enough, I was driving all across southern California to meet his various family members, sisters and cousins and nieces and nephews. Every occasion, I looked around with a blank stare on my face, waiting for the disapproval of everyone.

Ian was everything to me. He taught me how to live outside of my bubble back here in America. He taught me a lot of things, but the biggest gift he gave me was showing me how worthy of love I was.

Watching him eat was enlightening. There were days he ate hardly anything at all while other days he ate upwards of 4,000 calories. He never hurt himself while eating. He had no correlation between exercise and food. He responded when his body told him he was hungry, but I could also watch him eat two bites of something, recognize he was not actually hungry, and step away. His relationship with food was intuitive and fluid, offering me a new perspective on the world.

As a result, I had my first interactions with true intuitive eating. I learned that intuitive eating didn't mean eating anything and everything I wanted, as Minnie Maud previously taught me. By this point, I clearly saw how Minnie Maud could incite binging tendencies for some, while for others, it gave food freedom. Thankfully for me, I was one of the lucky ones and found small moments of food freedom in Minnie Maud. Being with Ian taught me that intuitive eating was about listening to cravings coinciding with the nourishment I knew my body needed. That meant frozen pizza and broccoli. Or hot sausage and corn. It meant lots of ice cream and Christmas cookies, but it also meant learning to find my sweet spot with alcohol. My eating habits became a long, arduous process of actively listening; to not only what my body wanted, but what it needed. Only then did I start to make decisions that were both compassionate and educated. I started to care about my body as a whole unit. I stopped putting my mind and body on opposing sides and instead merged them together to find common ground.

I knew if Ian was meant to be in my life, he would never have it easy. However, given the happiness that I felt while with him, I felt an impulse to actually try—to not always be so ridden with disordered thoughts. There is this concept floating around suggesting that you cannot love others until you love yourself. The phrase is thrown around like every other clichéd idiom the gurus of social media cling onto, so much so that I bought into it without processing what that really meant.

Ian, however, made me show up in the real world, recognize that I was underweight, and do something to change it. Ian, with his sweet soft soul, never forced me to do anything. He sat and listened when I wanted to talk, asked questions, and genuinely tried to understand. He recognized he couldn't fix me, and he never tried.

As our relationship progressed, we talked less and less about my anorexia, and more about life in general. Essentially from two months into our relationship, we lived together. Popping back from either of our units, I learned to find comfort in sleeping next to him, feeling the warmth radiate off his body into the night. I grew to admire and love how he fell asleep mid-sentence, after resting his head on the pillow for less than five minutes, while I stayed up for hours on end, looking at the ceiling, outlasting the nightmares that awaited me if I gave way to slumber myself.

Late into most nights, we laid in bed exchanging childhood moments, forgotten dreams, and hidden fears. He taught me what healthy sex was supposed to feel and look like. He was so patient. We absorbed one another, voraciously, as though we knew one day our time together would come to an end, all the while hoping for a different outcome.

In the two years we shared together, my biggest hurdle was understanding I deserved him. It was a battle I overcame, only to falter days later. He always stood ready to remind me, though.

About eight months into our relationship, we both needed to find an apartment to live in. We sat at my desk, legs tangled, as he toyed with my fingers.

"Where should we live?" he asked.

I let a few moments go by, swimming the words around my mouth before I responded with my own question.

"You want to live with me?"

I don't know what sort of reaction I expected from him. He stopped playing with my fingers and looked straight into my face with an almost hurt look.

"Of course I do. I love you." He paused, "Do you want to live with me?"

"I think I do. I'm just scared you won't like living with me. I'm not easy."

"You've said that since day one, and I only continue to love you more with each new day. I love you so much. I want to build a life together."

And just like that, we found an apartment and moved in shortly thereafter.

People go on and on about how you need to love yourself before you can love another human being. For me, that wasn't true. I respected myself, but I didn't love myself. Loving Ian showed me how to love myself.

Our relationship was never perfect. Both of us had our faults, as imperfect humans always do. I will love him until the day I die, and I know he will always be in my life. Because of him, I am a changed, stronger, softer human being.

No one can make you recover. I have made that statement more times than I could ever count, and I stand by it. Ian did not make me recover. He did, however, show me there was a different way to view myself. He saw value in me in a way I previously couldn't fathom. He stuck by me.

By the end of our relationship, we both had lost sight of who we were to one another. Caught up in the daily grind of finances, working jobs while finishing out school, dealing with the fact that neither one of us ever really got the approval from each other's families, struggling to find middle ground on political issues we both found vital to our character—we had a lot working against us. I see that now. But our love was beautiful.

Ian is an incredible human being. I only wish the absolute best for him, and I hope he is an imperative friendship in my life for as long as I walk this planet. Because of him, I learned what I am worthy of, both in love and in life. He encouraged me to always seek out my own happiness, regardless of whether that included him or not. Oh, how I wish we could have worked.

Ian is a soulmate of mine. I don't believe in soulmates in the traditional sense; I believe each of us have many soulmates spread throughout our lives that we may or may not come across. Ian is a soul mate of mine, just as my best friend Emily is a soul mate of mine. No matter what occurs—the trials, the arguments, the distance—these soulmates will linger in my heart, and I in theirs. Ian and I will always share a piece of our lives with one another, and I know because of him, I am a better human being.

He opened up a part of the world I never thought possible for me. Ian showed me I was capable of loving another human being, as well as being loved. I had cut myself off from that for so long. I viewed myself as damaged, unworthy of love. He spent the entire two years

of our relationship slashing any self-directed slander I
uttered.

Finding faith in hopelessness.

LEARNING ABOUT VARIOUS RELIGIONS around the world opened up my life outside of the narrow scope of anorexia and recovery. Previously, everything was about those two things, but when I found my passion in studying religion, everything changed.

My thoughts are not my own. This concept is often spattered around every self-help book, constantly quoted on Instagram. It's taken me years to understand, but I want to qualify this statement by saying that while my thoughts might not be my own, I am responsible for the reactions and modifications I make of them. I need to objectively observe every thought that enters my head.

A lot of people favor anthropomorphizing their eating disorders as though it is a different person inside of their head. I don't usually like this concept because I think, at a certain point in my recovery, I could have very easily utilized this as a way of displacing blame. *"Oh, it's not me, it's ED. I'm not trying to do this."* I think that, in the depths of one's disorder, there is not a lot of control because yes, the person is incredibly disordered and it is a relentless nightmare to break out of. However, I—now years and years into my recovery—should not be using that as an excuse. It took me a great deal of time to switch this, but for me, it has worked.

I view each and every thought I have as something outside of me. Instead, each thought is something I "hear." I keep it objective. No thought comes from me purely. Just like most concepts in the world around me are not what I created. Everything I know has been taught to me, apart from the intuition I'm growing more and more accustomed to. But that has nothing to do with my thoughts; that has to do with my emotions. I'm talking about thoughts related to decisions and actions and things I ultimately will be responsible for. Thoughts are how I view the world and also how I react to it. When a thought enters into my head, I have the ultimate power to accept it, reject it, mold it, transform it, or forget it.

Obviously, this took years and years of shaping my mentality, but now, I am somewhat capable of it. When I was fourteen years old, I really was not capable of taking the thought, *"I'm a damaged, broken, disgusting pig for having sex with that man,"* and turning it into something valid and real, like, *"That foul man raped me. I did not deserve that."* This is something I am only capable of doing now because I took years and years to craft this in me. It also has a lot to do with studying the various religions of the world.

I respect and honor Christianity entirely. While I have my issues with it, I love and respect the beautiful tradition of Christianity. I think my specific childhood of learning Christianity gave me a preconceived notion on how to view my body that ultimately hindered my ability to adequately recover. When I stripped away from the barriers of the mindset I was taught, I viewed my body as more than this vessel of purity to protect.

Each new religion I studied opened up a way of thought I clung onto. Though the courses focused primarily on the secular study, inevitably the mind gravitates toward attempting to find a way of embracing a faith. Studying these ideas in such a deep, intense manner practically begs you to give it a shot. In many of my courses, we focused on eastern religions and philosophies, and in them, there is an emphasis on the life cycle, such as in Buddhist thought; samsara, meaning birth and rebirth. Aging and death come with the territory of being alive. One only needs to accept this truth; suffering derives from feeling attached to the change of the body. There is no one on this earth beyond this very truth; we all age, we all die. We are all subject to the same fate, regardless of the faith you subscribe to or reject. Rather than fear the changes, letting go allows for life to keep the intoxicating glow it should have. I mean, how utterly beautiful is it to be alive?

If anything, above all else, what I learned in studying English and religion in conjunction with one another is that our lives are shaped by the narratives we construct. We curate stories in our mind, and those stories serve two purposes. First, these narratives help us conform to society, no matter how authentic we strive to be, we falter in selling the idea of who we are to others because it, naturally, is hard to invite isolation into our lives. It simply and truly is easier to be like everyone else.

Second, these narratives help us sleep at night, however morbid that might be. When I half-assed my recovery, I told myself I was doing great because to confront the truth meant I was actually still actively allowing myself to die. Those aren't thoughts that settle within my mind kindly. Those thoughts kept me up at night. So, instead, I told myself I was making progress. To seal it as a normal, valid thought in my mind, I had to portray that externally. I had to have others believe me, too. The narrative, though created within me, had to fit someone else's opinion of me as well. If it does not convince more than one person, the narrative fails to perch into existence. It was only once I acknowledged this that I made any real progress. I learned this concept in a course focused on the faith and hope. This course broke my entire being. It taught me that we choose to have faith in these narratives, clinging to the hope that they will all work out. We tell ourselves these dreams about our lives, forcing them to exist as truth, if for a moment, based on the idea of faith or hope.

I used to have faith I would somehow miraculously recover from my eating disorder. I used to have faith I would forget about the harm I have caused my family. I used to have faith in a relationship. I desperately wanted the relationship to work. At the time, I deemed it a personal representation of my faith. I wrote that very sentiment down in a journal. Then, it was like writing down my feelings for my boyfriend incited off a series of cursed events. I stuck with it, as I did and always will believe good relationships are durable, but I was miserable for well over a year. Looking back, I feel naïve. I was so wrong and blinded by so much. I look back now and see that my relationship had nothing to do with faith. Crafting a healthy relationship, receiving true forgiveness from my family, actively recovering from my eating disorder, all require a hell of a lot more than simply believing in this nuanced, warped idea of what our world considers "faith." Faith is actually entirely irrelevant.

During my final semester of university, that course on faith and hope utterly shook me. In this course, I learned of the concept called the "ethical universal," which is outlined in Soren Kierkegaard's book, *Fear and Trembling*. Without going down too much of a philosophical wormhole, the ethical universal is, essentially, the cultural norms, values, rules, and social roles people conform to in order to not feel "othered," or set apart. Basically, it deals with the status quo, but on the basis of morality rather than fitting in. At my core, I am a people pleaser and in my life, I have often succumbed to going above and beyond in order for people to like me. That's why I stayed in dead-end jobs, friendships, and relationships for months after their expirations dates—because I was sucked into "hoping" everything would work out.

Ultimately, though, I've learned that "hope" is a dangerous, dangerous, *dangerous* concept. Hope weakens me. Hope allowed me to stagnate through life because I could put my desire for change into this apathetic concept of hope. Hope is lazy. I am inactive when I hope because I'm waiting for something else to do the work. I put up with everything around me I was unhappy with because I personally didn't want to deal with the hassle of separating shared items, shared history, shared dreams. I could easily sugar coat all of this by saying I wanted to work on my failed relationship because I "believed," in us, but if I'm being honest, I know I'm a sucker for a good ethical universal. It bleeds into every aspect of my life. I always felt aware of the societal status quo I tried to embody, but somehow labeling it as the ethical universal and putting it into religious context really resonated with me, in a harsh, yet enlightening way. It was in this course, I learned I don't want to always exist in the ethical universal, especially when it holds me back. I would like to have more courage and will than that.

For me, ever since I was in high school, religion has played such a central but nuanced role in my life. In taking this class, I felt like I understood and truly got at the root of faith. Growing up with Jesus plastered everywhere in classes, I grew wary of anyone who made it seem like believing in Jesus was the end-all, be-all to a content life. When I was raped, everyone around me could tell something within me changed. When the damage manifested into my anorexia, teachers constantly told me I was able to pray away the pain. No. That's bullshit. Sure, Jesus might be the son of God. He might be Christ. I don't want to negate the possibility of that in the slightest. But having faith in that concept isn't going to do anything about the trauma I experienced and the trauma I live within every day. All my life, I struggled to comfort myself in both faith and knowledge. I looked for external approval in every manner possible. Is it even possible to find solace in either? In my four years of college, I witnessed various professors teach me such startling facts about different religions, and yet they will tell me in private conversations they subscribe to that very religion.

Hope is perilous; it incites uncertain comfort in us as individuals. I can't just hope for things to get better or wish them into existence. That incites apathy, which is the characteristic in others I most abhor. I did not get to where I am today with baskets full of coins as I passed by wishing wells. I worked hard to recover from my eating disorder and gain the sixty pounds back I needed to sustain my health. I didn't hope I would magically wind up one day without the fear of foods. It required (and still does) the diligent, daily task of forcing myself to eat like a normal human being, knowing it would become routine, therefore easier. If I relied on hope, I would surely be dead. I am certain of it.

Having faith and hope, per common terminology, lends itself to manipulative rhetoric. Faith is so much higher than the anachronistic definitions left up to interpretation in scriptures and sermons. Faith is about a single person grappling with the fear of the unknown and *then* completely giving him or herself over to that unknown, trusting it will all work out, though all signs point to the contrary. Faith is choosing the terrifying act of hope.

I understand I'm young. Being that I'm only twenty-two years old as I write this, I have experienced few deaths. I'm no stranger to grief, though. Especially after studying it in university; grief is something I think often of.

I will never become accustomed to people dying. I will never become accustomed to losing what I loved. When something I love is no longer around, no matter the circumstances, it breaks me. I will never want it to not matter to me. I don't want a placid, stoic heart that allows for people to pass away from me without care. I want every moment of grief to linger in me like a scar. These scars are the story of that relationship and the love for that person. It is a testament to the existence of caring for one another. If I have to bruise and batter myself over the pain of losing someone, so be it. It is worth it. To love is worth anything and everything.

Grief comes in bouts, swirling around like I'm stuck tumbling down a hill or creviced in a tornado. As I spin, all I can see is the wreckage swindled and caught up in the dust. Everything floats. I see the grave magnitude of the world, struck by all its beauty and allure. I see parts of the world that no longer exist as a result of the tornado. I keep spinning and I see fragments of the decay and I hold onto that. I see its memories. I see the person as they spin and float alongside me. All I have to do in this moment is float. Floating keeps me alive.

The tornado spins without care for me, merciless and perilous. I don't see an end, so I continue to float. I have no time to catch my breath because I just keep spinning. As time wears on, though, the spinning slows; it doesn't quite halt, but it slows. I begin to breath. I begin to function again. I never know when the next turbulence will hit or what causes it, but I learn to live again. Months trail on, and I find I know when to expect the next tornado to hit. I expect, I prepare, I take it head on. I don't always jump over the whirling decay, but even when I don't, I know I come out of it on the other side, with a few more bruises but a lot more hope.

This is how I came to view my eating disorder and the days where relapse feels luxurious. One of the grandest achievements in my recovery was when I fully released myself of the anorexic identity. I had to let go of defining myself by my recovery, by my struggle, by my blog. I had to move beyond that and grieve for it. I know on the outside, grieving an eating disorder sounds like the dumbest thing, but for years, my eating disorder was the one thing in my life that felt like an invested, best friend. It felt like God. I had others around me that cared, but no one understood. Not their fault, it's the trouble with the mental illness. It's how it succeeds, because it has an innate ability to ostracize itself from everyone who can eat healthfully, or at least, semi-healthfully.

Stripping away the power of beauty.

AS I PREPARED FOR MY FINAL YEAR of college, I set my sights on finding a new job, one more directly tied to the career path I envisioned for myself. That meant constantly applying to various educational jobs, such as tutoring, youth outreach, student teaching, and anything of the like. A few weeks into what appeared a fruitless endeavor, I cleared out the search bar on the job site I browsed, just to see what would pop up near my location.

I scrolled and scrolled, finding jobs that sounded like an utter bore or I was critically underqualified for. Then, I saw a job posting marked, "Bridal stylist." Intrigued, I clicked on the link and gave the job description a quick glance.

Just as every other young gal, I grew up watching *"Say Yes to the Dress,"* and had a romanticized idea as to what the process entailed. However, I read through what the job required, and something about it struck a chord with me. I started to think about all the brides that diet for the wedding and go to severe extremes just to fit into a dress, and I wondered if I could change that. I knew I single-handedly wouldn't revolutionize the wedding industry with a newfound body positivity phenomenon, but I felt compelled to see if I could bring anything to the table. And anyway, I needed a palate cleanser from writing a different iteration of same, "I'm so passionate about teaching," cover letter I sent off to everyone. For this cover letter, I surprised myself by the words pouring out of me. I wrote it in a matter of minutes, looked it back over, and felt really good about it.

I was honest as can be. I wrote about my recovery, what body image meant to me, and what I hoped to gain out of working for a bridal store. Low and behold, I received an email back asking me to come in for an interview.

At the time, I was with Ian, and I laughed as I told him, "I got a job interview at the bridal store."

"Really?" he said. "Actually, I think you'd be so good at that."

"Humph," I responded to him, contemplating whether or not I'd go. "I have no actual experience relevant to the job. There's no way I'll get hired."

I wavered on the issue for a few minutes, then decided it couldn't hurt to check it out. An interview was an interview, and no one can deny the need to practice interviewing.

A few days later, I found myself in an open warehouse: cardboard boxes scattered everywhere, exposed pipes, gray cemented floors, and a sparkling silver mantled wall. With two folding chairs set up in the middle of the showroom, I sat with the CEO of the company. In the corner of the open room, a woman stood opening up boxes and pulling out dresses.

For an hour, I sat there with him, sharing my story, telling him how much size inclusivity matters, expressing my concerns for these poor brides. Societal pressures are at an all-time high for brides, and if I can alleviate a bride's stress for the hour I'm with her, reminding her that she is beautiful as is, then all of my recovery was worth it. I didn't know it at the time, but I meant those words more than anything. I was very clear: I had no retail, no fashion, no sales, no bridal experience—absolutely nothing about me, on paper, looked fit for the position. But, I made it clear, *I would love every single person who walks through that door, and I would do everything in my power to help them see how "enough" they are.*

Thankfully, I landed upon a kind, compassionate CEO who only wanted the same thing for the brides. He took a chance on me that altered my life completely. Little did I know that woman in the corner would also change my life in more ways than I could ever express. The job itself taught me more about recovery and how to exist in this world than I ever thought possible as well.

Some things I learned and recognized about weight, weight gain, and body image while working at a bridal store:

- A person's weight is irrelevant to his or her worth.
- How much a person weighs is quite literally the most boring part about him or her.
- When quality people are intrigued by you, it is because certain, innate, desirable characteristics shine through you. Those meant to enhance your life will never stick around because of your appearance.

Most women on their wedding day will be the thinnest they have ever been and ever will be. When the title of "bride" is given to a woman, it's as though they retain a new mentality, one capable of more stamina, more willpower, especially when it comes to managing weight.

Inundated with Pinterest and bridal magazines, all women see during their engagements are perfect figures in these gowns that expose models' tasteful cleavage, smooth, tanned backs, windswept curls, and so on. Everything online about weddings is curated to look as perfect as possible. The pressure on brides retracts a lot of the enjoyment one should feel during what is supposed to be a magical time in her life. Instead of celebrating this motion to declare a couple's love in a permanent, dedicated symbol that is marriage, brides are compelled to spend the

months leading up to the wedding burdened with stressors
that negate the entire experience.

The wedding industry is a mess. Just like society,
it's ridden with manipulative lies begging women to feel
inadequate. The standard of beauty is narrow, with
margins slimming down more and more it seems.
Representation for women of color is practically
nonexistent and often, companies post weddings of LGBT
members only because they feel like they have to. If a
woman is not the ideal of society, chances are she will find
no quality images she can research in preparation for her
wedding day. Too bad the society's manifestation of
perfection isn't even attainable—instead, it's filled with
wild airbrushing and boundless Photoshop.

One of the first questions I ask a bride I'm
partnered with is, "Are you excited?" This is after I've met
the friends and family she chose to bring with her and have
scooped her away for a private moment in the fitting room.
Rarely do I receive a flat-out, "yes," to that question. My
brides always qualify a yes with a, "yes, but I'm nervous."
More often than not, the reply is, "I'm just nervous," or, "I
hope the samples fit," or, "I hope I look okay in the
gowns."

And every single time, these responses break my
heart. It does not matter if the bride is a size 0, 10, or 28—
brides of every size come in with these reservations
because they feel like they have so much to live up to.
What should be a fun, light-hearted, gal-pal session is often
turned into two hours of self-loathing and anxiety.

It no longer surprises me to see a bride pick herself
apart, cry, and feel so defeated in a gown that I, as a
complete stranger, would gawk at her beauty in. Usually,
families encourage and build the bride up, rejecting all of
the negative words she says. I stand by her and do the
same, hoping that something in our honest, loving

comments lands with her. The absolute last thing that should be on a bride's mind as she is walking down the aisle is whether or not she has a stomach pooch. I don't know if I always help, but I try my hardest. I spend all day long trying to right the wrongs of our repugnant society. I hope I make a bit of difference. If a bride feels beautiful in the time I have spent with her, regardless of if she finds her dress with me or not, I have done my job. I truly mean that.

Finding a wedding dress is an emotional purchase. It is so much more than a woman putting on a gown, looking in the mirror and feeling like a bride. I've found that helping a woman find her perfect wedding dress requires that woman to look in the mirror, feel encouraged about the life decisions she's made and feel *"enough."* She needs to look in the mirror and not be overwhelmed by the beauty of a dress, but by the beauty of who she is, in body, spirit, and mind.

I treasure my time with my brides. I get to learn about their lives, their careers, their love, and who they are at their core. I fall in love with each woman before me, so when they critique themselves, I get worked up. I'm known to cry with a bride over society making them feel like they are anything but perfect in that very moment. As I stare at them, staring at their own figures, I picture the eighth grade version of them. I wonder who hurt them as children. I wonder how they came to be the women they are. I think about if they struggled picking out graduation gowns, or prom dresses. I hope they learn to look beyond the need to feel perfect aesthetically.

Brides are constantly repeating the same phrases, *"I want to lose x amount of pounds before my wedding,"* or, *"Can I order a size down because I'm not where I want to be?"* and every time, I just want to board us all on a spaceship so we can lie elsewhere, at a planet that doesn't make us feel so inferior.

Working at this bridal shop, in turn, healed a lot of my own body image problems. As I witnessed so many brides attempting to change their bodies, I thought a lot about myself.

Changing my body to fit what society wanted could make me feel better. Sure. Yes. That was and still is true. I could lose ten pounds, and people may begin to praise my appearance. But then, I think back to what I've learned working at the bridal shop: my weight is the most boring aspect of who I am. If I expended my energy on what society wants me to look like, I'd find my value in my vanity. Then, I'd build my self-worth around this newfound appearance. I'd then have to work toward maintaining this newfound appearance.

This upkeep would then control my life. I would have to live in a state of mind that meant constantly watching not only my food intake and exercise regime, but also the shifting perspectives on society's ideals of aesthetics.

A few years ago, thigh gaps held the obsessions of many, however now, it's all about thicker thighs and tiny waists. It all constantly shifts. I could chase these ideals all my life, working my body to fit into the molds of society. It might make me feel better, but how long does that last? The ideal will change only months later, and I'm back on the chase. I might receive a small moment of satisfaction from the flippant comment of someone else, but then I'll play the waiting game for the next compliment, surviving on only other people's value.

As I see brides always on the hunt to look better, I saw firsthand how pursuing what our culture aesthetically approves of is the furthest idea of anything sustainable. It almost always leads to disappointment. I myself chased after this for so long, only to be met with disappointment and a fully-fledged eating disorder that stole years of my life away from me. That's what the wedding industry and just basic diet culture is, essentially; a collage of empty promises veiled by Photoshop and faulty rhetoric convincing us otherwise.

I had to accept that a body ideal was not something I could chase after anymore. If I wanted to be content with who I was—just as Julia and nothing more—I had to accept my body as how it naturally wanted to be. I had to accept a form of body image that had nothing to do with loving myself, but rather about not caring about what I saw in my reflection. I had to learn how to be body neutral, to look at myself in the mirror, catching my stomach at a bad angle and choosing to shrug my shoulders rather than tilt my head and shoot hateful comments toward myself.

I don't have to love my body, and I'm not sure that I ever will. I know many people will utter these words, but for me, that was never the point of my recovery. My recovery was never about loving my body; my recovery only truly succeeded once I began to separate my worth from my body entirely.

I had to come to a less painful, more peaceful place with my body while also learning to care for and appreciate how my body carries me through this world. I never set out to love my body or place worth in it. That, I learned, is wasted energy. My body is meant to lead me toward a meaningful life, one where I'm stronger, brought to an intellectual level of stimulation, not existing on a purely physical identity of worth.

Having poor body image meant my energy was consumed with thinking about only my weight, but nothing further. The less energy I exert toward those useless thoughts allows for more energy toward creating a fulfilling, purposeful life. It means more energy can be spent conversing, reading, writing, exploring, and living in this world.

Giving up the idea of body image is *work*. It is not easy. It is taxing, time-consuming, and a bit dire when all I see as a young woman is everyone around me trying to look different than who they are. The thoughts for me still exist—they haven't gone away thus far. I am years into the process, so I cannot guarantee or shed the hint of a promise that they will disappear, but I've found that detaching myself from the thoughts is the key to overcoming the struggle.

By the same token, I discovered that it was possible to focus too much on overcoming my battle with body image. I found myself listening to podcasts, reading medical journals, reading blogs, writing my own blog, and curating my social media presence in such a way I was surrounded by only body positive activists, but it felt like I kept myself living in this body-centered world rather than being able to think about the other things of this world I wanted to.

The work is so important, not just for our own mental health, but as a social justice movement. I say this not to minimize that; please know that. However, I've learned that more often than not, I needed to just live my life, engage in hobbies and with people that having nothing to do with body image or eating disorders.

In the beginning of my recovery, I needed complete immersion in this messaging for my healing. But sometimes, listening to and reading all of this informed content too often continued to perpetuate the hyper focus on body and food. It was refreshing and cathartic to step away from it all.

In the time I spent writing this book, I lost and regained ten pounds. Then, I gained fifteen more pounds. This year tested me with losing friendships, financial burden after financial burden, and a few toxic situations I didn't know how to get out of. Every time I sat down to work on my manuscript, I felt the pangs of my past, creeping up and haunting me. Having the opportunity to write this book is an immeasurable blessing, but I never realized how rehashing this part of my life would affect me with such magnitude.

Crafting these chapters forced me to confront parts of the past I assumed I previously overcame, only to realize I had in fact not. Over the course of writing this book, I noticed behaviors swerve back in. I started looking up restaurant menus to pre-plan meals. I bought a scale. I started drinking diet soda again.

In the first draft of this book, I didn't address this. It wasn't until I uploaded the document to an email to my editor and pressed, "*send*," I realized where my headspace was at. The more I thought my eating disorder, my mental illness gained power. A relapse felt viable.

If I could give one piece of advice to anyone out there struggling with an eating disorder; the most important thing is to forget about your eating disorder. Get out of the recovery community online. Don't indulge in the eating disorder, in any capacity. That's how it lingers. That's how it prevails.

I fear many people reading this book will find themselves disappointed by the lack of information on my actual recovery. Somewhere along the way though, I realized I couldn't write that again. Not here. That would be a disservice. That would be harmful. Instead, I treat this book as an homage, bidding farewell to a part of me I no longer wish to entertain.

For me, recovery and a healthy body image lies in when I think about food and my body last, after everything else. Meaning, I'm too busy living a fulfilling life to put more energy than necessary toward these things.

For a really long time, I didn't want to look like myself. This is an integral factor in me getting the eating disorder in the first place. I didn't want the body that I had when I was abused. This, though it took me years to admit to myself, was the exact reason why I had an eating disorder in the first place.

These moments of inadequacy manifested in other ways, too, that I only fully realized several months ago. I dyed my hair blonde and used Sun-In forever. I completely changed the type of clothing I wore. I stopped braiding my hair. The girl that was raped had her hair in brunette braids, weighed more, and wore dresses all the time. Years passed where I was a straight-haired blondie who only wore leggings and hovered at a weight too low for her own good. I subconsciously was doing all of this because I desperately wanted to become a separate entity from the girl who was raped. I "othered" myself, though I know that is impossible. I wanted to forget about the girl who all that trauma happened to and simply become a new person with a clean slate.

It's only in recent months that I stopped putting lemon juice in my hair, relaxed on the eating, and discovered my personal style again that I realized, even if I could completely separate myself from the Julia who suffered from an eating disorder and was so terrible and cruel to everyone around her, I wouldn't want that. She taught me how to endure and overcome strife. She taught me how to be hard, but also how to break down and be soft and see the world again. I would never be as empathetic as I am now had it not been for what I endured, and it felt so cruel to my own self to want to forget everything I have done to become the woman I am. So, if you see me now, you'll see me as I am, rather natural. I wear less makeup now. My hair is back to the color I was born with. I no longer want to "other," myself. Instead, I'm letting her fold into the place in my heart she always belonged. She is my heart.

In the past year, a lot of changes sprouted, bringing with it the need to fully seek out what the next steps of recovery looked like. I then asked myself the question of whether or not I'd transition from "recovering," to, "recovered."

Making peace with food is exhausting, daunting, and nearly impossible to conceive. In fact, it very well may be impossible to achieve. I know I have difficulty in writing this book because I don't know how to jot down the process of my recovery without failing to do the justice of the tears and night sweats. Oh, the night sweats.

It also doesn't all go away. Parts do. I know now that when my body screams at me to think only of my softer thighs touching one another, I can redirect those thoughts. I know how to acknowledge them. I know how to invalidate them. I know how to move on and continue to feed myself even as my legs squish against the wood panels of the chair. I know now I can't rely on protein bars to fill me up so I don't have to spend time throughout my day eating.

What doesn't go away is living in this world drowning in diet culture. Coworkers will continue to swap diet tricks, trading paleo for keto. People will swear up and down about the magic benefits of intermittent fasting or eating raw vegan. One day sugar is the devil, and the next day, it is all about gluten abstinence. No one wins. Everyone loses. Capitalism thrives.

One of the fallacies of recovery is that it is so easy to think and believe that everyone in the recovery community no longer feels affected by these messages of propaganda. Sure, I cannot speak for others; they might experience true freedom and the ability to completely ignore these bated promises of diet culture. For me, though, there is always that question of intrigue: what if this new thing really is the answer? What if this is the cure we all have been waiting for? What if this is the thing I really can do, even with my disordered past? What if this is the method of eating that allows me to maintain a socially approved body without torturing my own mind. The intrigue lingers, even though my eyes are opened to the manipulations that prey on us all.

Recovery means making the daily choice to nourish and care for myself, but it also requires the daily choice of choosing to no longer participate in diet culture. This has made me lose friends. I kid you not, I have had to hold so firm to rejecting diet culture, I've turned people off from being friends with me. But you know what? I grieved the friendship, but felt much better for it. There will come a time in your recovery journey where you will understand that it is okay to be selfish. It is okay to choose yourself when others choose themselves. Diet culture may serve them; it likely won't, but let them find that out for themselves. We cannot save everyone and especially in recovery, you need to save yourself and only yourself. Let others reach out when they are ready.

When you see people successfully thrive off diet culture, remind yourself that you are you and they are them. They did not lead the life you did. They do not have the same struggles. It's like this: I can have three beers on a casual night out, and I'll be fine. A little bloated and a little slower the following day, but I don't wake up absolutely craving more alcohol. There are people in my life, people I hold so dearly close to my heart, who cannot have a sip of alcohol without going on a dark path. I will never understand that, but I have to respect that, just like the people in your life need to respect your struggle and attempt to understand. I will likely never understand alcoholism to the degree I understand eating disorders, but I do my best to listen and show up when those who struggle need me.

When I find myself in conversations about dieting and weight loss, I get angry. I'm angry that we are bombarded with this system of inadequacy. This system that demands and demands, and takes the money of people who work so hard, all for the purpose of making ourselves smaller. It harms us all, whether we choose to participate in the game or not. If we choose to abstain, we are judged by the majority. We cannot win. So, I get angry. I overcompensate with my anger. This is not the right response.

The right response is compassion. I need to have compassion for the victims of diet culture. By doing so, I remind myself of my own pain of when I was trapped in the same cycle of dieting and body hate. Dieters are doing the best they can with the knowledge, support, and self-worth they have in those moments. All I can do is offer a different perspective, one of grace and care and slowing down to appreciate oneself.

So, no. I don't want your skinny teas. I don't want the body wraps. I want to look in the mirror and feel neither here nor there. I just want to look at myself and think, *Look at me.* I, Julia, I made it. I made it through it all.

Privilege

IN YOUR MIND, PICTURE SOMEONE with an eating disorder. What do they look like? Probably, even before reading this or knowing who I am, you pictured someone just like me. Young, already thin per societal standards, white, doing fine financially, and undoubtedly female. Also, though you're probably not thinking about these demographics, the person you're envisioning is also heterosexual and cisgender.

I am a part of this problem, so I'm taking this chapter to write about aspects of recovery far and beyond more important than my actual journey. If you take anything from this book, it is this chapter and this chapter alone.

Recovering from an eating disorder is the hardest thing I have ever done. I will never be one to say it was easy. That said, I *did* have it easy. I am years into this, and though significant progress has helped me become a much stronger woman, my eating disorder still plagues my thoughts, albeit in different, quieter forms now. My recovery required constant, tedious, daily, hourly work of rewiring my brain, negating disordered thoughts, and choosing opposite actions. I poured my soul into recovery and still do.

This book is a failure if anyone walks away from reading this and thinks I am the one who worked hardest in this struggle. My second chance at this world came about in the midst of hundreds of privileges denied to many, yet simply handed to me.

Eating disorders can and do happen to anyone. The world fails to recognize this, though with the continual presentation of eating disorders portrayed in characters in the media just like me. Take for example the 2017 film *To the Bone*, which starred Lily Collins. If you don't know who she is, Google her. We could be cousins. Collins plays a twenty-year-old, upper-middle-class, white, heterosexual, cisgendered female who has immediate access to a well-established group home paired with a top doctor for eating disorder recovery. As a result of no one addressing eating disorders in mainstream conversation, any representation is few and far between to begin with, but the examples we do receive are inadequate in full, honest representation. Instead, it fuels irresponsible stereotypes, leaving so many people who deserve recognition and the simple act of being heard un-diagnosed.

Eating disorders, and most specifically anorexia, are framed as a mental illness happening only to people who look like me. An already-thin, white female.

Had I wanted to go to treatment or been medically compelled to go, my family would have found a way. Perhaps not without financial stress, but my parents had the capability to make it happen. Going through this, I was oblivious to the ease with which I had access to treatment options because all I wanted was to naively ignore the possibility of anything like that. Had I needed to or had a change of heart, though, the very next day I would have been at treatment center. This is an option denied to not just many, but to the majority.

According to the National Eating Disorders Association (NEDA), the average cost of eating disorder treatment is $28,000 a month. *A month*. Let's take a moment to remember that my weight restoration process in and of itself lasted ten months. That's almost $300,000, not to mention the additional costs of travel and other incidentals. Recovery doesn't end after the weight restoration ends; in fact, I'd argue that is almost when it begins. Additionally, that same research had findings express that only one out of ten sufferers of eating disorders receive treatment. This is not because they are like me and stubborn, but because most people literally do not have the option of going.

Rather than focusing on the success of my own recovery, which I spent far too many chapters addressing, I need to make space—valuable, honorable, recognizable space—for those who are not heard right now.

I had it easy. People clearly saw I was unhealthy because I dropped down to an emaciated, skeletal weight. My eating disorder would have been just as dangerous had I not lost a pound. The physical deterioration I did to myself could have (and likely should have) killed me at any weight. So many people do not receive any sense of concern from others because people are so quick to look at someone's physique and make value-based judgments on that solely.

Our society is obsessed with the idea of progressing. We are not allowed satisfaction or contentment. We always must strive for more. This mentality quickly seeps into how we view our bodies, always fixated on areas we could improve based on what the media portrays as ideal—living in this culture of counting calories or finding the next fix. Constant dieting conversations forces anyone in recovery to feel like a failure for partaking in behaviors specifically rejecting the cultural norms. Coupled with existing in a marginalized body (aka, someone above what society considers a healthy weight), choosing to participate in recovery and eating more and eating food that typically incites fear is even more difficult.

Thinness in our world is equated to health. No one can swerve around that fact. We are making small steps toward rewiring this ingrained concept, but on the surface, almost all of us look at the people around us and will base what we assume their health status as based on how much they weigh. I fall into this trap, too.

That person you pictured—the thin, white, heterosexual, middle to upper class, cisgender female—is only a portion of those affected by eating disorders. Thinking that this type of person is the only person makes no space for people in larger bodies, people of color, people of different genders, people with disabilities, people who struggle financially, etc. That person makes no room for people who wake up every day and have to explain an area of his or her identity to others just to justify his or her existence.

During those initial few months of finding my footing in recovery, I found the stigmatization others had surrounding eating disorders difficult enough to navigate. I felt so much shame for it. Now, years into this and learning more about the world around me, I have no hope for the version of myself who also had other identities to combat. I know myself, and I know I would not have been strong enough for that. I have immense, monumental respect for anyone who recovers from an eating disorder or at the very least embarks on the journey, but I look to my other sufferers who have such a further uphill climb and weep for the oppression they face.

It is important for me to write this book for a number of reasons. Sure, one is so that I can take ownership of my story. I do think writing these chapters out and mulling over different memories helped me heal and really move on from some of the trauma I have experienced. Honestly, though, I needed to write this story for anyone out there who feels like recovery is impossible. That is the main reason why I wrote all of this out. But, even more so, I need others to know that I am not the only type of person who gets an eating disorder. We need to make space for people who don't look like me. My hope is that someone who doesn't look like me or identifies with me can read this and find the courage to share their story, because their story is so needed right now. I am able to pop onto Netflix, type in anorexia, and the movie that shows up has a main character who literally could be my sister.

Even online, in the shared space of recovery—the place I felt safest—I reflect back on this time and realized how void of diversity it all was. Of course, my recovery started in 2013, and the world is in a far different place now, here in 2019, but my goodness, we have so much more to go.

The myths about eating disorders are proliferate, one being that eating disorders are solely about weight loss.

Drops of Jules

I AM ALMOST TWENTY-THREE YEARS OLD. I've experienced twenty-two Christmases, been in three car accidents, traveled to nine countries, earned two degrees, written two fictional novels, lived in eight different homes, helped over three hundred women find their dream wedding gowns, and broken two hearts. This past year was arguably the most transformative, even more so than when my recovery first began. I found a job I am over-the-moon passionate about. I am more in love with my job than most brides feel when they find their actual dress. I spend each day learning women's stories and making them realize how beautiful they are without changing a single aspect of themselves. How special is that? It's not my forever, but it's my now, and I feel so blessed.

Six years ago, I embarked on a journey, questioning the destination, wondering if there was an end. Now, I sit here, at the end of my story, living in a brand new city by myself, working full-time, socializing more than I ever have, going out for drinks, waking up early to write instead of run, barely having a moment to myself, and I know more answers than I thought I ever would. I am able to move on.

There is no denying that recovery is the hardest trial of my life thus far. I've come to realize that is largely in part due to the fact that recovery infiltrates every aspect of strife. Recovery rooted itself in my sexual abuse trauma, in financial stress, in navigating healthy relationships and sometimes failing. Six years ago, I honestly believed I would not make it my twenty-second year of life. I wondered if I would be alive, because I didn't believe I deserved to be alive. By saving grace, I found a community, a sense of support and strength. Around the world, I had people encouraging me to push forward, to continue on. People joined me in eating pints of ice cream. Together, we celebrated challenging fear foods. We demolished our dismay together. We grew resilient together. I let people into my life. Though this started through social media, the true and right kind of community found me in the real world, which was immensely beneficial in those final clinging ideas of recovery.

Countless times, I learned I am stronger than I give myself credit for. I surrounded myself with people who helped me come to those realizations and gave me that final push. I easily could have lived a relatively normal life at 85 percent recovered. Now, I don't want that. I want it all. I can taste it. It's within reach. I will settle for nothing less.

Going full force into the last parts of recovery meant sacrificing a lot of the disordered behaviors I found a sick, deceitful comfort in. This meant grieving these clouded coping mechanisms. The strangest and most beautiful part about that, though, is that now here I am, and not one part of it felt like a sacrifice.

I genuinely say I am happy. I feel happy. Life is moving forward and falling into place. It is fast-paced and chaotic, and yet, it feels really right.

For a long time, questions bubble under the surface of my heart. Most, I refused to actually acknowledge or answer. With the chaos in the world right now, I cannot avoid them anymore. Vulgar, obscene chaos. It's erupted within me suppressed anger. Anger, you see, because it begs the questions I always refrained from asking myself:

Who could I have become?
Who would I be if he had not hurt me?

Who would I be if I did not know her?

Who would I be if I had not squandered years of my life damaging the very relationships that stuck by my decrepit, battered mind? For years, I avoided the question as I was under the impression that who I could-have and would-have become was someone better. Believing that assumption made me cower in an unhealthy shroud of shame. I didn't always acknowledge that, but this chaos in the world made it an inevitable confrontation.

Whoever the hell I would have been? Had all of the grime not happened, she would not be me. Plain, simple, and clear. I tried to make myself a different person altogether but that turned me into the very monster I wanted to avoid.

Here I stand—still a mess—but a stronger, defiant mess. A mess that is here to survive for better days ahead. A mess that is occasionally quite proud of the progress she has made.

I get asked a question by others a lot, and I've always found it simultaneously thought provoking and healing to consider: If I could go back and prevent the former, younger version of myself from having anorexia, would I?

Honest answer?

No.

Would I love to take away the pain I caused my family? Absolutely. That I would do in a heartbeat. I would do everything to take away all the frustration and worry I planted in them. But, I wouldn't stop myself from having anorexia.

I look back and mourn a lot for the wasted months and even years of my life, but I don't regret any of it. Having an eating disorder was simultaneously the worst and best thing that ever happened to me.

As a result of my anorexia, I cultivated hundreds of friendships around the world, connecting with others who have struggled. Together, we persevered. Together, we learned how to exist once again. Over the years, I have met so many people who followed my blog, and we shared our journeys with one another. We shared how we went from living in dark existences, convincing ourselves that was enough, to going out and enjoying beers together. This formative time in my life served as a testament to the hell I and so many others out there endured and the battles we conquered.

Growth and recovery are not linear. Here I am six years in, and I still figuring it out. It does get better though, and it is so worth fighting for.

For anyone out there actively suffering, whether it is binge eating, bulimia, anorexia, anorexia athletica, orthorexia, or disordered behavior that currently doesn't fall into a prescribed category (but is still so valid), know this—you are worthy.

Let this serve as a reminder: recovery is possible.

Not only is it out there waiting for you, but it will be worth more than I could ever articulate.

I don't have all the answers for everyone out there. All I can do is sum up what I learned along the way, and what I grew to understand recovery as.

- Recovery is not IIFYM.
- Recovery is not working out 7 days a week.
- Recovery is not counting calories.
- Recovery is not coffee for breakfast.
- Recovery is not secret exercise.
- Recovery is not two-a-days at the gym.
- Recovery is not researching menus before going to a restaurant to find the lowest calorie item.
- Recovery is not weighing myself.

- Recovery is not denying myself another piece of pizza when I am still hungry.
- Recovery is not staying in to surf the internet when my friends are out.
- Recovery is not Diet Coke after Diet Coke after Diet Coke.
- Recovery is not constantly hating my body, but it is also not constantly loving my body other.
- Recovery is not food shaming other people.

Our world is so quick to categorize; to set everything in stone. Black or white thinking. There are no gray areas allowed. We like to feel set apart. We like labels. We like the idea of an "other." If I've learned anything over these past six years of recovery, it is that I abhor labels. I reject labels. I don't want to be Julia, the runner; Julia, the Broadway fanatic; Julia, the recovered anorexic. Heck, I don't even want to be Julia the writer. These are all just parts of me. They should *not and* don't define me.

I just want to be Julia.

I learned that being *just* Julia is more than enough. It's me. It's who I am holistically and emphatically. That is what is right. That is who I need to be. That is who I am. I no longer choose to live in extremes. My goal for myself is to find my own intuitive, mindful way in this world. For anyone else out there that has had an ounce of resonance with my story, my hope for you is the same. Use your voice. It has so much worth.

Acknowledgments

To Sparklle Rainne, for the immeasurable, undeserving patience she bestowed upon me. I never anticipated writing this book to hurt and heal so much, but you gave me so much grace.

To all of my coworkers, I apologize for grunting at you all every time you asked me how the progress on this book was. Rather than ceasing to ask, you found gentler, easier ways to have conversations about the book that rejuvenated me.

To Sophie Koplin, because you deserve a special note. You made me feel heard and valid. You reminded me why I write and why I healed.

To Emily Brennan, for you are not spoken of in the book enough, but only because you played the most subtle, yet most significant role in my recovery. You helped me become a person outside of my disorder. You also showed me and continue to show me what having inner confidence from a broken soul looks like. You are my first and forever soulmate.

To Thom Babbes, because though I am the worst at keeping up in connections, I need you to know that you are who I think of when I think of people who supported me in recovery. You gave me chances to thrive when I deserved them, and you also held me back when you knew I didn't. You didn't let me walk over you. You pushed me to get better. To you, my gratitude is unbounded.

To Bradford Kierkegaard, for lighting a fire within me. Without you, I'd never have the reverence for religion.

To Michael Caldwell, because you are a clever asshole who challenged me more than any other professor.

You shook my entire narrative, but I am a better human being for it.

To Anna Comerford, who found me in a time of transformation, gave me the opportunity to shine, and never let me get a big head as a result. If I have never met you, I surely would be a lot quieter and a lot less healed. You are always right, and I will spend the rest of my life calling you for advice. I like the idea of reincarnation, purely because it means you get a chance for the world to treat you better. You, out of every single person in my life, deserve a chance for the world to give you a kinder life.

To Public Square Coffee House, who let me linger at their tables for hours on end and subsequently hooking me on their huckleberry tea. Your smooth jazz, amiable servers, and expensive tea fueled me through the holiday months when I felt lonely and lost in the first draft of this manuscript.

CPSIA information can be obtained
at www.ICGtesting.com
Printed in the USA
BVHW090040230719
554057BV00015B/746/P